National
Association of
Purchasing
Management

National
Association
of Purchasing
Management

Purchasing's Organizational Roles and Responsibilities

by

Harold E. Fearon, Ph.D., C.P.M.

and

Michiel R. Leenders, DBA, FPMAC

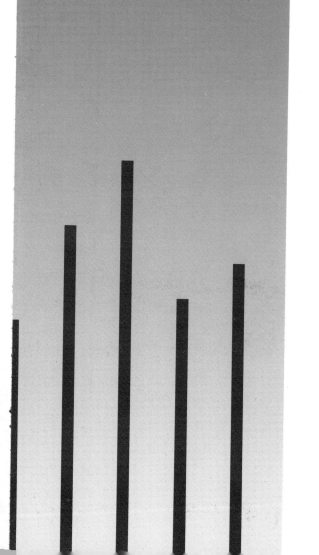

PURCHASING'S ORGANIZATIONAL ROLES AND RESPONSIBILITIES

by
Harold E. Fearon, Ph.D., C.P.M.
Director
Center for Advanced Purchasing Studies

and

Michiel R. Leenders, DBA, FPMAC
Purchasing Management Association of Canada
Professor of Purchasing Management
Western Business School

ACKNOWLEDGMENTS •

The Center for Advanced Purchasing Studies wishes to thank the purchasing executives in the organizations who provided the data on their organizations. Eight purchasing executives assisted in the design and testing of this questionnaire. Their inputs resulted in significant improvements. These advisors included Gene Haisting at Honeywell, Tim Coats at Pillsbury, Roger Cox at 3M, Tom Lee at General Mills, Tom Lang at Computer Devices International, Steve Wilkie at Molson Breweries, Anders Nordin at Abitibi-Price, and Doug Knox at Northern Telecom.

Furthermore, a special group of reviewers examined the draft manuscript. This group included

Michael G. Kolchin, D.B.A., C.P.M., Lehigh University
Heinz Bauer, The Bauer Group
Stewart L. Beall, C.P.M., Cyprus Amax Minerals Co.
Nancy C. Cummings, C.P.M., American Airlines
Robert Dunn, Bank of America
Leonard J. Garrambone, NYNEX
Bonnie J. Keith, ABB
Helmut F. Porkert, Ph.D., Bayer Corporation.

At CAPS, Jennifer Richelsoph, Debbie Wagner, and Carol Ketchum assisted in the various phases of this research, paying proper attention to the logistics and data input.

Akshay Kumar wrestled with the inevitable bugs in the computer programs and emerged a tired but clear victor.

At the Western Business School, Sue LeMoine was responsible for the proper presentation of the text material.

As co-researchers we take full responsibility for the final study results and hope they will make a significant contribution to the field.

Harold E. Fearon   Michiel R. Leenders

ISBN: 0-945968-25-6

CONTENTS •

TABLES AND APPENDICES •

EXECUTIVE SUMMARY •

This report is based on data collected in May 1995 from 276 U.S. and 31 Canadian organizations in 21 industry groups. Of the 307 organizations, 43 (14%) had 1994 sales of less than $500 million; 54 (18%) had sales of $.5 billion to $1 billion; 117 (39%) were in the $1.1-billion to $5-billion sales category; 47 (15%) in the $5.1-billion to $10-billion sales category; and 44 (14%) had sales of more than $10 billion. This study updates the first research project ever undertaken by CAPS: *Purchasing Organizational Relationships*, published in 1988.[1] This earlier research covered 297 U.S. organizations. A total of 118 U.S. organizations participated in both the 1988 and 1995 research, affording a unique opportunity to trace changes within these firms. Key findings from this 1995 research are:

1. The majority of organizations (65%) were organized on a centralized/decentralized basis, in which some purchasing is done at the corporate headquarters as well as at major operating divisions/plants. Twenty-three percent had a centralized function in which all or almost all purchasing is done at one central location. Only 12 percent were decentralized, in which purchasing was done on a division/plant basis. Service organizations tend more towards centralization (32%) than manufacturing organizations (20%), but only 3 percent of service organizations are decentralized versus 15 percent of manufacturing companies. Canadian companies tend to have more centralization (39%) than U.S. companies (21%). Companies under $500 million in sales tend to have more centralization (33%) than those over $10 billion (18%). Within the organizations that participated in both the 1988 and 1995 studies, 60 percent retained the same purchasing organizational structure, but 40 percent changed.

   For firms with multiple business units, 52 percent had a headquarters purchasing department plus business unit purchasing departments; 27 percent had a headquarters purchasing department plus personnel in the business units who released against contracts; 12 percent had a headquarters purchasing department only; and 9 percent had only business unit purchasing departments. In organizations composed of a single business unit, 63 percent had one purchasing department, 30 percent had a headquarters purchasing department plus other purchasing departments, and 7 percent had multiple purchasing departments but no headquarters purchasing department.

2. The purchasing function reports to the president in 16 percent of the organizations and to the executive vice president in 15 percent. The most common reporting relationship is to a senior/group vice president (19%). Other reporting relationships are to a manufacturing/production/operations vice president (15%), financial vice president (10%), to an administrative vice president (9%), materials/logistics vice president (7%), and engineering vice president (1%). Eight percent report elsewhere in the organization. Compared to the 1988 report, the reporting line to a senior/group vice president was new and substantial at 19 percent. One surprising finding from the doubly researched group of firms was that 66 percent changed reporting line since 1988.

3. Functions reporting to purchasing include scrap/surplus disposal (63%); materials and purchasing research (60%); inbound traffic (51%); stores/warehousing and inventory control (both 41%); material planning (40%); outbound traffic (39%); receiving (35%); other (27%); quality assurance (25%); and in-plant material movement (19%). All of these percentages represent significant increases over those reported in 1988.

4. Professional staffing levels averaged 89 people for all organizations, ranging from an average of 11 persons for companies in the smallest size range to 289 for the largest organizations. Support staff for all organizations averaged 58 people, ranging from an average of 6 for the smallest firms to 251 for the largest. Service organizations tend to employ fewer staff and the ratio of professional to support staff is about half as high (.36) as it is for manufacturing companies (.71). Purchasing staff levels in 1995 compared to the 1988 study showed substantial decreases; the decline from the 1988 average of professional staff of 118 people to 89 people in 1995 indicates almost a 25 percent decrease.

---

[1] Harold E. Fearon, *Purchasing Organizational Relationships* (Tempe, AZ: Center for Advanced Purchasing Studies, 1988), 58 pages.

During the past 12 months, only 15 percent of the respondents increased the size of their purchasing staffs, averaging about a 10 percent increase. However, 41 percent downsized, averaging about a 14 percent decrease. Expectations for the following 12 months show a significant turnaround. Increases and decreases appear to be almost in balance.

5. Purchasing's current involvement in major corporate activities shows outsourcing as the only activity with a moderate involvement. Particularly low were government relations, international counter-trade/offset planning, marketing planning, and corporate mergers/acquisitions/alliances.

6. Typical communication media between head-office purchasing and purchasers located elsewhere rated telephone as the highest (4.3), fax (4.0), and e-mail (3.7), well ahead of personal meetings (3.0), tele-conferencing (3.0), and letters (2.8). Videoconferencing is slightly used currently (2.0).

7. A ranking of current role/responsibility/ involvement of corporate headquarters purchasing in selected activities shows the following six activities as most common:

   1) establishing policies and procedures (4.3);

   2) contracts for common requirements (4.1);

   3) purchases head-office requirements (4.0);

   4) collects and provides purchasing information (4.0);

   5) participates in system-wide purchasing/supply personnel decisions/actions (3.9); and

   6) develops supply systems (3.9).

   All activities showed increased involvement expected in the future.

8. The popularity of teaming and participative approaches to supply management indicated the following ranking for the top four choices:

   1) cross-functional teams (3.6);

   2) commodity teams (purchasing personnel only) (3.1);

   3) purchasing councils (purchasing managers only) (2.9); and

   4) teams involving suppliers (2.9).

9. Data about the chief purchasing officer (CPO) showed:

   a) **Title** — Vice president (37%); Director (36%); Manager (21%).

   A very wide range of titles currently are in use. For the doubly researched companies, 59 percent changed titles since 1988.

   b) **Age** — The average age was 50.

   c) **Education** — 95 percent held at least a bachelor's degree; 39 percent held an advanced degree.

   The bachelor's degrees were: Business (58%); Engineering (19%); Liberal Arts (12%) and Other (11%). These percentages were almost identical to those of 1988. The most common graduate degree is an M.B.A. (70%) or Master's in Management (12%); 6 percent had Ph.Ds.

   d) **Years in Present Position** — 6 years, the same as in 1988.

   e) **Years with Present Employer** — 18 years, the same as in 1988.

   f) **Years of Functional Experience** — Purchasing (16.3); Operations (4.6); Other (2.1); MIS (1.0); Engineering (0.9); Accounting (0.9); Marketing (0.8); Finance (0.7); and Traffic/ Distribution/ Logistics (0.3). These figures are somewhat different from those in 1988, with MIS showing the largest percentage increase.

10. The largest change expected by 2000 is in the area of integrated systems development (47 percent).

IMPLICATIONS •

This 1995 study repeated many of the questions reported in the 1988 CAPS report but also attempted to address a broader range of relevant issues. Thus, the following comments will partially focus on comparisons to the earlier study and partially on new findings. Clearly, different people will not interpret the data the same, and cause and effect relationships are not proven by this type of research. Nevertheless, it is hoped that the data, and these comments, will be helpful to executives in charge of various purchasing activities as well as to researchers in the field.

1. The most popular form of purchasing organization in larger companies is the centralized/decentralized option. Since 1988 the popularity of this form of organization has grown even further. Even though, in the aggregate, organizational forms may show the same pattern, the 118 companies, which participated in both studies, showed that 40 percent had changed their organizational structure since the previous study. Perhaps a sort of life cycle exists for any of the organizational options. Perhaps restructuring is required with some regularity to deal with new challenges and clear away old organizational cobwebs that accumulate if the structure stays static too long.

2. Chief purchasing officers (CPOs) report to senior executive vice presidents in 34 percent of all companies surveyed. Presidents/CEOs account for another 16 percent and other vice presidents account for the remainder. Compared to 1988, 66 percent changed reporting line! The new addition for this study "senior/group VP" at 19 percent had the largest single category of reporting line. In the 1988 study, the manufacturing/operations vice president had the most common reporting line (24%). In this study this reporting line decreased to 15 percent. Obviously, many organizations have changed reporting relationships and purchasing has often switched to a more-senior vice president.

3. Functions reporting to purchasing are increasing. Since 1988 all functions listed have increased, showing a broader range of supply-related functions as part of purchasing. The increases have been greater on the manufacturing side than on the service side, bringing the two closer to one another. Even though scrap/disposal still leads the pack at 63 percent, many others are also close, and traffic

and quality assurance have shown particularly large jumps. Perhaps it is the more universal acceptance of the materials management concept that is evident here, as well as the move towards more-integrated logistics.

4. Professional staffing levels fell 25 percent from 1988 levels and support staff often support two professionals. The downsizing of this last decade still is not completely over for purchasing organizations. Clearly, fewer people are being asked to do more work. To what extent computerization has affected this trend is not clear from this research.

5. The literature on strategic purchasing has strongly advocated that purchasing be significantly involved in major corporate activities beyond supply. The research data do not show that this actually is taking place. Even outsourcing, which obviously should require major procurement input, is shown as having moderate purchasing involvement and is the only corporate activity that obtained even a moderate ranking. Thus, a major challenge for purchasing in becoming more involved in organizational activities of a strategic nature still lies ahead.

6. Communication media between purchasers show the popularity of fax and E-mail. It will be interesting to see whether videoconferencing will replace personal meetings.

7. Headquarters purchasing groups are heavily involved in policy and procedures establishment, as well as corporate-wide purchases. These findings were no great surprise. The relatively low-ranking of involvement in training may reflect the recent tough economic times, but also a major issue for the years ahead. Compared to most functional areas, purchasing tends to require relatively few staff. Ensuring that supply staff are well trained and continuously improved is vital to effective procurement performance and should require significant headquarters purchasing involvement.

8. Participative approaches to assure a lower total cost of ownership; shorter new product/service to market time; better quality; and greater synergy between customers, suppliers, specifiers, and purchasers have been highly publicized during this

last decade. Empowerment and team building have been touted as the new wave of improving both motivation and results. Typical procurement initiatives in this class include various forms of teams involving other internal functions, suppliers, and customers. The research showed, however, that currently use of these approaches was relatively low, although significantly increased use was expected in the future. Perhaps with the downsizing of the function and the need to meet current organizational requirements, the opportunity of spending extra time on activities such as these teams has been minimal.

9. The chief purchasing officer (CPO) is a different breed today from the one identified in the 1988 study. Still well educated, the current CPO operates under a very wide range of titles, although vice president is the most common one. The background shows a wide range beyond purchasing, far greater than in the previous survey.

   Perhaps this reflects the tendency in a number of organizations to move executives from a totally different background like MIS, engineering, or accounting into the top slot in purchasing. In larger organizations, the appreciation that the prime skill of a CPO is one of management rather than purchasing may also be behind this move. It is difficult to argue that purchasing executives should move to other top executive positions without leaving the door open for the reverse.

10. This last decade has been a tough one for many organizations, functions, and individuals. Difficult economic times, international competitive pressures, and significant political, social and environmental concerns all have left their mark. The purchasing function, and those who work in the supply field, also have been influenced. Downsizing continues. Supply has become leaner and meaner. Fewer people have a wider range of greater responsibilities, and future expectations are for more of the same. Obviously, many executives are wrestling with these challenges, and innovative solutions need to be found, although managing well what we already know cannot be overlooked. Many initiatives already are under way, with integrated systems development as the most common challenge. Increased procurement effectiveness is vital to organizational success.

REASONS FOR THIS STUDY AND ITS DESIGN •

The Center for Advanced Purchasing Studies (CAPS) undertook this research project for five reasons:

1. The question of how purchasing is organized to meet the challenge of contributing effectively to company goals and strategies is as relevant and important today as it was almost a decade ago. Business people and academics need current, accurate information on various facets of purchasing organization and operation by corporate size and by industry.

2. It always had been the intent behind the creation of CAPS to provide a series of "base lines" through its studies, which could be revisited in future years. Indeed, it is this unique continuity feature of CAPS that permits it to undertake projects and longitudinal studies that individual academic researchers would have great difficulty mounting.

3. The first study ever undertaken by CAPS: *Purchasing Organizational Relationships*[2], also turned out to be its most popular publication. The authors of this 1995 study believed that, because of the high interest in the topics addressed and the significant changes in North American industry over the past eight years, such an update and expansion was necessary. Prior to 1988 almost no research into purchasing organizational relationships had been done and certainly not on the scale undertaken by CAPS.

4. It was also recognized that the 1988 study did not address a number of areas of significant interest in 1995 such as (a) greater detail on the roles, responsibilities, and communication means used by headquarters purchasing organizations in centralized/decentralized organizations; (b) the use of councils and teams, co-location of purchasing personnel and consortium buying; (c) the role, responsibility/ involvement of purchasing in major corporate activities; (d) the staffing levels of professionals and support staff in different purchasing locations; and (e) information on the degree of involvement and trends in the above four areas.

5. The procurement executives who participated in the March 1995 Executive Purchasing Roundtable session in Tempe, Arizona, strongly suggested that the 1988 predecessor of this current research be updated and expanded.

SPECIAL FEATURES OF THIS RESEARCH

Two special features beyond topic coverage for this study were:

1. The opportunity to go back to a number of the organizations who participated in the 1988 study and to examine what significant changes have taken place.

2. The inclusion of major Canadian organizations allowed for a greater geographical coverage.

THE RESEARCH QUESTIONS

The fundamental research questions for this study remained the same as in the previous study. What are the responsibilities of those charged with executing the supply function in large companies, and how is the function organized? Who is in charge, using what title, and what is this person's background?

It was important that this second study into organizational relationships conform as much as possible to the 1988 study. Therefore, the basic questions dealing with the size of firm, titles, background of the chief purchasing officer (CPO), reporting line, responsibilities, organization and size of the department were kept essentially the same.

As could be expected, the temptation to go beyond the original study was too strong. Since the majority of firms in the original study indicated they used a combination of centralization/ decentralization in organizing the function, it was believed that it might be useful to explore the details within this organizational form further. Furthermore, questions were developed indicating the number of purchasing professionals and support staff located at the head office as well as elsewhere, nationally and internationally.

---

[2] Ibid.

The means of communication between various business groups were also investigated, as was the involvement of purchasing in major corporate activities. An attempt also was made in this study to establish a degree of involvement as well as a perceived trend. Lastly, Canadian organizations were included in this study to ensure coverage of the total North American continent north of the Mexican border.

Not all of these efforts turned out to be totally successful. Some of the respondents were confused with the question about multiple and single business units, and some questions were not answered by all respondents.

The Questionnaire

Fifteen key question areas required a five-page questionnaire, designed to be filled out in about 15 to 20 minutes. A copy of the questionnaire is included in Appendix B. Eight purchasing executives in the U.S. and Canada were field tested on a draft design of the questionnaire, which resulted in significant improvement in the clarity and detail of the questions.

The Sample

In May 1995 eight years after the questionnaires for the original organizational relationships study were sent out, 602 questionnaires were sent along with a cover letter and stamped return envelope. The 556 organizations in the United States were selected from the *Fortune* 1000 list and comprised 21 industry groups. In Canada, companies were selected from a list supplied by the Purchasing Management Association of Canada (PMAC). No governmental organizations, banks, or retailers were included in this survey.

Questionnaires were sent only to organizations in that the chief purchasing executive could be identified by name and title. It was hoped that at least 200 usable responses would be obtained. Questionnaires sent to companies that participated in the previous study were given the same number as in the previous study for potential comparison as a subgroup of the total. The 46 Canadian companies were given a specific subset of numbers to allow for separation.

Of the 602 questionnaires mailed, 308 were returned by the data cutoff date, for a 51 percent return rate. Of the 556 mailed to U.S. firms, 276 responded for a 49.6 percent return rate. Of the original 297 firms who responded in 1987 to the first survey, 261 were mailed a questionnaire for this 1995 survey and 45 percent responded, yielding a sample of 118 firms who had responded to both the 1987 and 1995 surveys. On the Canadian side, of the 46 firms approached, 31 returns were received for a 67 percent response rate. The high response rate was most gratifying and certainly lends credibility to the data and analysis, even though not all participating firms responded to all of the questions.

DESIGN OF THIS STUDY

Table 1 presents the number of usable responses received for both 1995 and 1988 studies, by size of organization (by 1994 and 1986 sales revenue categories). Compared to the 1988 study, the $10-billion-and-over category increased from 9 percent to 14 percent of all responding firms and the under $500-million category decreased from 28 percent to 14 percent. On the Canadian side, 42 percent of the respondents fell into the $1-billion to $5-billion category and 23 percent in the under $500-million group.

TABLE 1
RESPONDING ORGANIZATIONS, BY SIZE,
FOR 1995 STUDY AND 1988 STUDY

Sales Dollars	1995 Study U.S.*		Canada**		Total		1988 Study	
	#	%	#	%	#	%	#	%
Under $500 million	36	13	7	23	43	14	84	28
$0.5 billion to $1 billion	49	18	5	16	54	18	45	15
$1.1 billion to $5 billion	104	38	13	42	117	39	110	37
$5.1 billion to $10 billion	42	15	5	16	47	15	31	11
$10.1 billion and over	43	16	1	3	44	14	27	9
TOTAL	274	100	31	100	305	100	297	100

* U.S. Dollars
** Canadian Dollars
Two firms did not supply sales dollar information.

Table A-1* presents the number of usable responses received broken down by 20 industry groups (plus one service group) and by size of organization in terms of sales revenue. The largest number of responses came from the services group (68 companies); electronics (51 companies); chemicals (31 companies); aerospace (27 companies); food and beverage (23 companies); paper (20 companies); and petroleum and coal (19 companies).

Low responses came from furniture and fixtures (1 company); instruments; rubber and plastics; stone, clay and glass; and tobacco products (all 2 companies each); fabricated metal; and textiles (3 companies each); apparel; lumber and wood; machinery except electrical; and printing and publishing (all 4 companies each).

This reduces confidence in the industry data for these 11 industry groups. It is recognized that a given firm may have divisions in more than one industry, and that assigning a firm to its primary industry group may have resulted in some less-than-totally-accurate analysis.

On a sales basis, the responding organizations were well distributed. The largest category included the 117 organizations in the $1.1-billion to $5-billion category; the lowest was 43 in the under $500-million sales category. An organization often includes a number of different divisions.

The respondents to the survey were promised complete anonymity. No individual organizations can be identified; only aggregate data are presented.

All data responses were loaded into a data base and the tables for analysis were prepared using Excel. Since the data are all in the data base, many additional cross comparisons, in addition to those presented in the body of the study, could be made. However, the need to keep the report relatively short required that the presentation of data be limited to three analytical formats: by organization size, by industry group, and by each of the specific industries. The major topics on which data were collected were:

Purchasing's Organizational Roles and Responsibilities

    Organization of the Purchasing Function

        - Of a Single Unit Firm

        - Of a Firm with Multiple Units

    To Whom Purchasing Reports

    Functions which Report to Purchasing

    Size of Purchasing Staff, and Changes, Past and Anticipated

    Purchasing's Role/ Responsibilities/ Involvement in Major Corporate Activities, Now and in the Future

    Communication Media in Today's Purchasing Organization

    Corporate Headquarters Purchasing's Role/ Responsibility/Involvement in Selected Purchasing Activities, Now and in the Future

    Purchasing's Use of Various Purchasing Techniques Now and in the Future

The Chief Purchasing Officer (CPO)

    Title

    Age

    Education

    Years in Present Position

    Years with Present Employer

    Years Experience in All Functional Areas

Major Changes by 2001

No salary information was collected, for two reasons: (1) that information is readily available from a number of sources and normally is updated annually, and (2) such information is sensitive in many organizations, requesting it probably would have reduced the response rate.

The data are analyzed and presented in four major groupings:

1.   By organization size, broken down into 5-dollar categories (1994 sales revenues).

2.   By each of the individual 21 industry groupings, for ease of analysis when one wishes to see the organizational pattern for a specific industry.

3.   By 1995 data versus the previous 1988 report, where such analysis was deemed relevant.

4.   By American versus Canadian firms, where appropriate.

---

* Tables whose number designations start with an "A" are found in Appendix A at the end of this report.

PURCHASING'S ORGANIZATIONAL ROLES AND RESPONSIBILITIES •

The purchasing function continues to evolve in the 1990s. The growing realization that corporate success requires superior performance from every function, including the supply side, has thrust the procurement area into a more strategic role. Historically, the evolution of purchasing during the past 100 years can be traced through six major eras:

1. The perception, during the early third of the century, that purchasing was primarily a clerical-type activity.

2. The shortage-induced attention of World War II (1939-1945).

3. The return-on-assets measurement influence during the 1950s and 60s.

4. The supply crises of the early 1970s, which saw severe world-wide material shortages and rapidly escalating prices.

5. The need to source globally during the 1980s to achieve the quality and cost levels required to compete with Asian manufacturers in the automotive and electronics industries.

6. The growing realization in the 1990s that purchasing must contribute effectively to organizational goals and strategies.

The February 20, 1995, *Fortune* magazine article, "Purchasing's New Muscle"[3] provides an interesting external viewpoint of the supply function and its current challenges. "What used to be a corporate backwater is becoming a fast-track job as purchasers show they can add millions to the bottom line" is the lead the author used to underline the article's message. Most corporate purchasing managers are well aware that they need to ensure that the supply function contributes effectively and strategically. Growing awareness by other managers of purchasing's potential will assist in further development of purchasing's contribution. Effective management and organization of supply is fundamental to assuring continuous improvement. This study provides current information on the roles and responsibilities major corporations have assigned to their supply managers and how, in turn, they have organized the function. This will not be the end. Continuing experimentation and evolution will result in further changes in the future. It is hoped, when enough of these changes have taken place CAPS again will provide the lead in researching the next round.

ORGANIZATION OF THE PURCHASING FUNCTION

Almost two-thirds (65%) of respondents in the 1995 study indicated they have chosen a centralized/decentralized type of organization for the purchasing function. This figure represents about a 10 percent increase over the corresponding 1988 data. Most of the increase came at the expense of centralized organization, which decreased from 28 percent to 23 percent over the same seven-year period.

In 1995, 21 percent of U.S. respondents had a centralized organization, versus 39 percent of the Canadian respondents.

The use of certain types of organizational forms for purchasing appears to be dependent on organizational size. Table 3 shows a steady progression, from 47 percent for companies under $500 million to 80 percent for those $10 billion and over for the centralized/ decentralized form of organization. The centralized version decreases for the same range of size of organizations, from 33 percent for the smaller companies to 18 percent for the largest ones. Decentralized organization is most used in organizations of $500-million to $1-billion sales range (23%) but is much-less used (2%) in the largest companies.

---

[3] Shawn Tully, "Purchasing's New Muscle," *Fortune*, February 20, 1995, pp. 75-83.

TABLE 2
**CENTRALIZATION AND DECENTRALIZATION OF THE PURCHASING FUNCTION,
1995 (U.S., CANADA, AND TOTAL), AND 1988**

Organization Structure	1995 Study						1988 Study	
	U.S.		Canada		Total			
	#	%	#	%	#	%	#	%
Centralized, in which all, or almost all, purchasing is done at one central location for the entire firm	57	21	12	39	69	23	83	28
Centralized/Decentralized, in which some purchasing is done at the corporate headquarters and purchasing also is done at major operating divisions/plants	180	66	16	51	196	65	175	59
Decentralized, in which purchasing is done on a division/plant basis	34	13	3	10	37	12	38	13
TOTAL	**271**	**100**	**31**	**100**	**302**	**100**	**296**	**100**

The most surprising changes since 1988 are shown below:

	1995 Under $500 million %	1988 %	1995 $10.1 billion and Over %	1988 %
Centralized	33	44	18	15
Centralized/ Decentralized	47	42	80	74
Decentralized	21	14	2	11

Interestingly, almost no changes have taken place in the $1.1-billion to $5-billion group in terms of percentage of organizations using each type of organizational option. That the aggregate figures remained the same does not indicate that no organizational changes took place during this period.

Organization Changes Within Firms

Since 118 companies of the total sample participated in both the 1988 and 1995 studies, an attempt was made to see if individual changes in organization had taken place, something the aggregate figures might not identify. Table 4 shows that a substantial amount of organizational restructuring has taken place, although the aggregate figures did not indicate such substantial changes.

For example, in the aggregate, these were the respective figures for the organizational form:

	1995 %	1988 %
Centralized	22	27
Centralized/Decentralized	68	61
Decentralized	10	12

TABLE 3
**CENTRALIZATION AND DECENTRALIZATION OF THE PURCHASING FUNCTION,
BY ORGANIZATION SIZE**

Organization Structure	(1994 Sales Revenue)											
	Under $500 million		$0.5 billion to $1 billion		$1.1 billion to $5 billion		$5.1 billion to $10 billion		$10.1 billion and over		Total	
	#	%	#	%	#	%	#	%	#	%	#	%
Centralized, in which all, or almost all, purchasing is done at one central location for the entire firm	14	33	12	23	25	22	10	21	8	18	69	23
Centralized/Decentralized, in which some purchasing is done at the corporate headquarters and purchasing also is done at major operating divisions/plants	20	47	29	54	80	69	32	70	35	80	196	65
Decentralized, in which purchasing is done on a division/plant basis	9	21	12	23	11	9	4	9	1	2	37	12
TOTAL	**43**	**100**	**53**	**100**	**116**	**100**	**46**	**100**	**44**	**100**	**302**	**100**

TABLE 4
CHANGE IN ORGANIZATION STRUCTURE BETWEEN 1988 AND 1995 (SAME 116 COMPANIES)

| Type of Organization Used in 1988 | Type of Organization Used in 1995 | | | | | | | |
| | Centralized | | Centralized/ Decentralized | | Decentralized | | Total | |
	#	%	#	%	#	%	#	%
Centralized	14	45	15	48	2	7	31	27
Centralized/Decentralized	9	13	54	76	8	11	71	61
Decentralized	2	14	10	72	2	14	14	12
TOTAL	25	22	79	68	12	10	116	100

Two firms did not supply the data.

However, Table 4 shows that only 45 percent of those centralized in 1988 were still centralized in 1995 and that 48 percent had switched to centralized/ decentralized. Of those centralized/ decentralized in 1988, 76 percent remained the same but 13 percent switched to centralized and 11 percent to decentralized. Lastly, of those decentralized in 1988, 14 percent remained the same, and 72 percent switched to centralized/ decentralized. Thus, of the matched responding firms, 70 remained with the same organizational form, but 46 switched.

Centralized/Decentralized Purchasing by Industry Group

Table A-2 presents the organizational data by industry group. The comparison of the 20 groups in the manufacturing sector and the service sector shows:

| | Manufacturing | | Service | |
| | 1995 | 1988 | 1995 | 1988 |
	(237 firms) %	(262 firms) %	(68 firms) %	(28 firms) %
Centralized	20	26	32	36
Centralized/ Decentralized	65	60	65	61
Decentralized	15	14	3	4

For industry groups with a reasonable number of responses, Miscellaneous Manufacturing at 71 percent and Food and Beverage at 52 percent were the two showing the highest concentrations of centralized procurement. Electronics at 82 percent, Paper at 75 percent, and Chemicals at 74 percent showed some of the highest percentages for the centralized/decentralized option. Aerospace at 27 percent had the highest percentage for the decentralized form.

Organizations with Multiple Versus Single Business Units

A further question not explored in the 1988 study tried to get a clear picture as to whether firms comprised of a single business unit organized differently from those with multiple business units. As might have been expected, significant differences existed, as shown in Table 5.

For multiple business unit organizations, 52 percent used a headquarters purchasing department plus business unit purchasing departments. Another 27 percent had a headquarters purchasing group plus personnel in the business units who released against contracts. On the Canadian side, 31 percent use a headquarters purchasing department only, versus 11 percent on the U.S. side.

In single business unit firms, 63 percent used one purchasing department, and another 30 percent had a headquarters purchasing department plus other purchasing departments. A surprising 7 percent had multiple purchasing departments without a headquarters group. For the U.S., 66 percent used only one purchasing department and in Canada it was 40 percent.

TO WHOM PURCHASING REPORTS

The reporting relationship of purchasing is highly relevant, since it is a sign of organizational status and a key to purchasing's influence within the organization.

TABLE 5
ORGANIZATION STRUCTURE OF PURCHASING, COMPARING THOSE HAVING
MULTIPLE BUSINESS UNITS WITH THOSE HAVING A SINGLE BUSINESS UNIT

Using Multiple Business Units	Percent of Firms Using		
	U.S.	Canada	U.S. + Canada
Headquarters Purchasing Department Only	11	31	12
Headquarters Purchasing Department, plus Business Unit Purchasing Department(s)	52	43	52
Headquarters Purchasing Department, plus personnel in the business unit(s) who release against contracts	28	13	27
No Headquarters Purchasing Department, but Business Unit Purchasing Department(s)	9	13	9
TOTAL	100	100	100

Using Single Business Unit	Percent of Firms Using		
	U.S.	Canada	U.S. + Canada
One purchasing department	66	40	63
Multiple purchasing departments, but no headquarters purchasing department	8	0	7
Headquarters purchasing department, plus other purchasing department(s)	26	60	30
TOTAL	100	100	100

This 1995 study found that some changes had taken place since 1988 as follows:

PURCHASING REPORTS TO:

	1995 %	1988 %
President	16	16
Executive VP	15	19
Sr. VP/Group VP	19	*
Administrative VP	9	13
Financial VP	10	7
Mfg/Prod/Opns VP	15	24
Mat'ls/Logistic VP	7	8
Engineering VP	1	1
Other	8	12

* Category not identified

Table 6 shows that the most common reporting line is to a senior or group VP at 19 percent, closely followed by the president at 16 percent, executive VP and manufacturing VP at 15 percent each, financial VP at 10 percent and administrative VP at 9 percent. It appears, in summary, that about 16 percent report to the president, about 75 percent to a vice president, and about 10 percent to a variety of other managers. On the Canadian side, the administrative VP was the most common reporting line (26%), followed by senior/group VP (23%). In Canada, only 7 percent reported to a president/CEO.

The comparison to 1988 shows a substantial decline in reporting to a manufacturing VP (from 24% percent

to 15%). This may be explained partially by the higher number of service organizations participating in the 1995 study. The inclusion of senior or group VP as an additional option in the 1995 study was a useful clarification; this turned out to be the most-common reporting line. On the Canadian side, significantly fewer managers reported to a president or executive VP, but higher percentages to a senior or group VP and a surprising 26 percent to an administrative VP.

Table 7 presents the reporting relationship by company size. For the smaller-sized group, in 19 percent of the companies purchasing reports to the president (up from 13 percent in 1988), 0 percent to an executive VP (down from 12 percent in 1988), 23 percent to a manufacturing/production/operations VP (down from 33 percent in 1988), and 19 percent to a financial VP (up from 7 percent in 1988). In only in 4 percent of the $500-million to $1-billion companies does purchasing report to the president (down from 16 percent in 1988). In the $5.1-billion to $10-billion range, 15 percent reported to the president (down from 32 percent in 1988), but 18 percent of the largest companies had a presidential reporting line (well up from 4 percent in 1988).

Table A-3 presents the reporting relationship by industry groups. For some of the largest-reporting industries, the relevant figures for 1995 and 1988 are:

Substantial differences are evident for specific industries between the 1988 and 1995 time frames. It also is clear that the senior reporting line, as evidenced by the totals, on the whole has increased substantially for these industries.

To Whom Purchasing Reports	1995 Study						1988 Study	
	U.S.		Canada		Total			
	#	%	#	%	#	%	#	%
President/CEO	47	17	2	7	49	16	47	16
Executive VP	45	16	2	7	47	15	54	19
Senior VP/Group VP	51	19	7	23	58	19	-	-
Administrative VP	18	7	8	26	26	9	38	13
Financial VP	28	10	4	13	32	10	21	7
Manufacturing/Production/Operations VP	44	16	2	7	46	15	71	24
Materials/Logistics VP	17	6	3	10	20	7	22	8
Engineering VP	2	1	0	0	2	1	3	1
Other	23	8	2	7	25*	8	35	12
TOTAL	**275**	**100**	**30**	**100**	**305**	**100**	**291**	**100**

*"Other" includes: Controller; Director - Business Development; Director - Materials Management; Chief Staff Officer; Materials Manager; Plant Manager; Director Commerical Transactions; General Manager, Director, Materials; VP - Shared Services; VP Manager of Procurement; VP Quality & Commercial Affairs; VP Supply Chain; Executive Director Operations; Senior Director - Materials Management; Site Manager; Personnel Manager; Executive VP Transportation; VP Mechanical; VP Human Resources; Controller; General Manager; VP Operations Support; VP Corporate Services; VP Controller.

TABLE 7
TO WHOM PURCHASING REPORTS,
BY ORGANIZATIONAL SIZE

	(1994 Sales Revenue)											
	Under $500 million		$0.5 billion to $1 billion		$1.1 billion to $5 billion		$5.1 billion to $10 billion		$10.1 billion and over		Total	
	#	%	#	%	#	%	#	%	#	%	#	%
President/CEO	8	19	2	4	24	21	7	15	8	18	49	16
Executive VP	0	0	8	15	22	19	9	20	7	16	46	15
Senior VP / Group VP	3	7	11	20	21	18	11	24	11	25	57	19
Administrative VP	3	7	3	6	8	7	6	13	6	14	26	9
Financial VP	8	19	7	13	14	12	1	2	2	5	32	11
Manufacturing/Production/Operations VP	10	23	14	26	14	12	4	9	3	7	45	15
Materials/Logistics VP	5	12	5	9	4	4	4	9	2	5	20	7
Engineering VP	0	0	1	2	0	0	0	0	1	2	2	1
Other*	6	14	3	6	7	6	4	9	4	9	24	8
TOTAL**	**43**	**101**	**54**	**101**	**114**	**99**	**46**	**101**	**44**	**101**	**301**	**101**

*"Other" includes: Controller; Director - Business Development; Director - Materials Management; Chief Staff Officer; Materials Manager; Plant Manager; Director Commerical Transactions; General Manager, Director, Materials; VP - Shared Services; VP Manager of Procurement; VP Quality & Commercial Affairs; VP Supply Chain; Executive Director Operations; Senior Director - Materials Management; Site Manager; Personnel Manager; Executive VP Transportation; VP Mechanical; VP Human Resources; Controller; General Manager; VP Operations Support; VP Corporate Services; VP Controller.

**Totals may not add to exactly 100 due to rounding.

PURCHASING REPORTS TO:

	1995			1988		
	President %	Executive or Senior VP %	Total %	President %	Executive or Senior VP %	Total %
Transportation	23	30	53	8	17	25
Paper	20	35	55	0	29	29
Primary Metal	20	13	33	31	15	46
Aerospace	19	16	35	18	24	42
Electronics	17	30	47	15	13	28
Services	12	52	64	24	21	45
Chemicals	10	27	37	13	19	32
Petroleum & Coal	10	5	15	9	18	27
Food & Beverage	5	59	65	32	19	51

Reporting Relationship Changes Since 1988

Table 8 shows for the companies who also participated in the 1988 study what changes in reporting line took place.

In the aggregate, the figures are:

PURCHASING REPORTS TO:

	1995 %	1988 %
President	14	16
Executive VP	15	18
Sr. VP/Group VP	17	*
Administrative VP	9	13
Financial VP	7	7
Mfg/Prod/Opns VP	18	24
Mat'ls/Logistic VP	6	8
Engineering VP	1	1
Other	13	12

* Category not identified

Therefore, on an aggregate basis, with the exception of the senior/group VP reporting line (not included in the 1988 research), it appears as if few major changes occurred. Table 8 shows quite a different picture, however. Only in about one-third of the companies did the reporting line remain the same and in two-thirds it changed since 1988. In combination with Table 7, this shows that within this group of 115 firms, at least 40 percent changed the type of purchasing organization and two-thirds changed the reporting line since 1988.

FUNCTIONS THAT REPORT TO PURCHASING

The specific purchasing-related activities that report to the purchasing function vary widely between different organizations. Table 9 shows the functions that report to purchasing in total and by the five size categories.

In descending order, the total percentages are:

	Percent of organizations in which function reports to purchasing	
Function	1995 %	1988 %
Purchasing	100	100
Scrap/surplus disposal	63	57
Materials & Purchasing Research	60	*
Inbound Traffic	51	40
Stores/Warehousing	41	34
Inv. Control	41	37
Material Planning	40	*
Outbound Traffic	39	31
Receiving	35	28
Other	27	27
Quality Assurance	25	16
Inplant Material Movement	19	*
Prod. Scheduling	7	*

* Data not collected

On the whole, this table shows increased responsibilities for purchasing across the board, with substantial increases in traffic, stores and warehousing, receiving, and quality assurance, when compared to the 1988 data.

TABLE 8
CHANGE IN REPORTING RELATIONSHIP OF CHIEF PURCHASING OFFICER
BETWEEN 1988 AND 1995 (SAME 115 COMPANIES)

| Person to Whom CPO Reports (1988) | Person to Whom CPO Reports (1995) | | | | | | | | | | | | | | | | | | |
| | President/CEO | | Executive VP | | Senior VP/Group VP | | Administrative VP | | Financial VP | | Manufacturing/Production/Operations VP | | Materials/Logistics VP | | Engineering VP | | Other | | Total | |
	#	%	#	%	#	%	#	%	#	%	#	%	#	%	#	%	#	%	#	%
President	6	31	3	16	4	21	3	16	1	5	2	11	0	0	0	0	0	0	19	100
Executive VP	3	17	2	12	5	29	1	6	2	12	1	6	2	12	0	0	1	6	17	100
Financial VP	1	13	0	0	1	13	1	13	2	24	0	0	0	0	0	0	3	37	8	100
Manufacturing/Production/Operations VP	0	0	4	15	6	22	1	4	2	7	11	41	1	4	0	0	2	7	27	100
Materials Management VP	1	11	1	11	0	0	0	0	0	0	1	11	3	33	0	0	3	34	9	100
Engineering VP	0	0	0	0	0	0	0	0	0	0	0	0	0	0	1	100	0	0	1	100
Administrative VP	1	8	1	8	0	0	3	23	1	8	4	30	0	0	0	0	3	23	13	100
Other	4	19	6	29	4	19	1	5	0	0	2	9	1	5	0	0	3	14	21	100
TOTAL	16	14	17	15	20	17	10	9	8	7	21	18	7	6	1	1	15	13	115	100

Three firms did not supply data.

TABLE 9
FUNCTIONS THAT REPORT TO PURCHASING
BY ORGANIZATIONAL SIZE, 1995 STUDY AND 1988 STUDY

| Function | (1994 Sales Revenue) | | | | | | | | | | | | (1986 Sales Revenue) | |
| | Under $500 million | | $0.5 billion to $1 billion | | $1.1 billion to $5 billion | | $5.1 billion to $10 billion | | $10.1 billion and over | | Total | | | |
	#	%	#	%	#	%	#	%	#	%	#	%	#	%
Purchasing	42	100	54	100	116	100	46	100	44	100	302	100	297	100
Production Scheduling	2	5	3	6	5	4	6	13	5	11	21	7	*	*
Material Planning	10	24	31	57	44	38	18	39	17	39	120	40	*	*
Receiving	9	21	27	50	34	29	15	33	20	45	105	35	77	26
Material & Purchasing Research	22	52	35	65	75	65	26	57	24	55	182	60	*	*
Stores/Warehousing	13	31	27	50	43	37	15	33	25	57	123	41	102	34
Inplant Material Movement	6	14	12	22	23	20	8	17	9	20	58	19	*	*
Inbound Traffic	15	36	35	65	61	53	19	41	23	52	153	51	120	40
Outbound Traffic	11	26	25	46	46	40	15	33	20	45	117	39	93	31
Scrap, Surplus Disposal; Inventory Recovery	19	45	37	69	83	72	26	57	26	59	191	63	169	57
Quality Assurance	8	19	13	24	23	20	15	33	18	41	77	25	48	16
Inventory Control	13	31	30	56	49	42	15	33	18	41	125	41	111	37
Other	9	21	15	28	30	26	15	33	13	30	82	27	81	27

* Data Not Collected   Companies Responding   302   297

Scrap, surplus disposal, and investment recovery still leads at 63 percent (after purchasing at 100%), closely followed by materials and purchasing research at 60 percent.

The logic for scrap/surplus disposal reporting to purchasing is that purchasing has knowledge of market demands and prices for scrap/surplus items and the communications channels through which information can be obtained. Performance of the inbound traffic function relates very closely to the purchasing decision on source, method of shipment, and overall cost/price paid, which accounts for the 51 percent that report to purchasing.

Incoming inspection is tied closely to the purchasing function. In the past, however, many organizations felt that it should be separated from purchasing so that the pressure to have items in-house on a certain date would not cause a compromise on quality standards. This study shows that 25 percent of the organizations have quality assurance/incoming inspection report to purchasing, evidently assuming that the purchasing decision-makers have a total understanding of the overall organizational needs and that the risk of compromising quality standards is not a major problem.

Functions Reporting to Purchasing by Industry Groups

Table A-4 shows the data by industry groups. A comparison between the manufacturing sector and the service sector shows wide diversity between five of the functions:

| Function | Function Reports to Purchasing | | | |
| | Manufacturing | | Service | |
	1995 %	1988 %	1995 %	1988 %
Scrap/Surplus Disposal	65	57	55	62
Inbound Traffic	44	30	59	45
Stores/Warehousing	59	31	67	62
Inventory Control	39	35	51	55
Outbound Traffic	32	29	49	3
Receiving	32	23	46	52

Evidently, the purchasing activity encompasses more functional areas in the service-type organizations than in manufacturing. This implies a broader role for the purchasing managers in service-type organizations. Since 1988 the gap has been narrowing, however, with significant changes in warehousing and stores and traffic in the manufacturing area, in particular. As might be expected, substantial differences exist between industries in the manufacturing sector with regard to functions reporting to purchasing. The figures in Table A-4 are clear in this regard.

PURCHASING STAFFING LEVELS

Staffing levels provide a further insight into purchasing's organization. In the 1988 study, information was gathered only about professional staffing levels. In this 1995 research, additional information was collected about head-office staffing levels as well as staff located elsewhere in the country and outside. It also was believed that support staff information would be useful, and so it was obtained.

Professional Purchasing Staffing Levels

Table A-5 shows professional staffing levels at *head-office locations* only for the 282 reporting companies. These data show that for 98 percent of all smaller organizations (below $500 million) the head-office professional purchasing staff consisted of 25 or less people. For those organizations with more than $10 billion in sales, 45 percent were in the 26 to 100 range, 28 percent were in the 25 or less, and 20 percent between 101 and 250. One of the reporting companies had head-office purchasing professionals in the 501 to 1,000 range.

Table A-6 shows for 181 reporting companies the number of professional purchasing personnel located *elsewhere in this country* (but not at the head office). For organizations with less than $1 billion in sales, these professional staffs, with only one exception, numbered 25 or less. As might be expected, as organizational size increases, more purchasing professionals are found outside head office, with two organizations reporting staffing levels in the 501-1,000 range.

Table A-7 provides similar professional staffing data for *locations outside the country* for 91 reporting organizations. The pattern is surprisingly similar to the data in Table A-6, even in absolute numbers in each category.

Table A-8 provides an overview of total professional staff in all locations. The averages for 1995 are particularly interesting when compared to the 1988 data:

PROFESSIONAL PURCHASING PERSONNEL:

Sales Revenue	Professionals (average)	
	1995 %	1988 %
Under $500 million	11	14
$0.5 billion to $1 billion	22	42
$1.1 billion to $5 billion	52	71
$5.1 billion to $10 billion	150	366
$10.1 billion and over	289	485

The obvious conclusion is that significant downsizing of purchasing professionals has occurred across all company size ranges. The biggest percentage decrease is shown in the $5.1-billion to $10-billion range at 59 percent and the smallest decrease occurs in the smallest company group amounting to 21 percent.

Support Staff Levels

Tables A-9, A-10, A-11, and A-12 provide data on support staff similar to that provided in the previous four tables on professional staff. The greater concentration in the lower staffing levels suggests that the ratio of support staff to professional staff, regardless of location, should be less than 1.0. This is confirmed in Table A-12. Since no data were gathered about support staff in the previous study, no observations about changes that have taken place can be made. However, it is possible to construct a summary showing current levels of professional and support staff by size of organization as follows:

Sales Revenue	Professional Support Staff	Support Staff	Ratio Support Staff Professional Staff
Under $500 million	11	6	.55
$0.5 billion to $1 billion	22	12	.55
$1.1 billion to $5 billion	52	27	.52
$5.1 billion to $10 billion	150	62	.41
$10.1 billion and Over	289	251	.87

This summary shows that support staff number less than professional purchasing staff in all company size ranges. In the up to $5-billion categories, close to 1 support person assists 2 professional staff. In the $5.1-billion to $10-billion range, 1 support staff assists 2.5 purchasing professionals. In the largest companies, 1 support staff supports 1.1 purchasing professionals. These figures lead to speculation as to why the $5.1-billion to $10-billion range would have proportionately the lowest levels of support staff, while the largest companies would have the highest. One possible explanation may well be that the largest companies use proportionately (to the sales revenue) fewer purchasing professionals than smaller organizations, but relatively more support staff.

An overview of all purchasing personnel average employment levels by organization size is provided in Table 10, giving a useful summary of Tables A-5 to A-12. Particularly striking are the support staff data for elsewhere within the country for the greater than $10-billion category. A support staff average of 259 for an average professional staff of 186 shows a ratio of 1.4 support staff per professional elsewhere within this country, compared to 52 per 105 or .50 at head office and 48 per 116 or .41 outside the country. This, at least, identifies the location of the high support staff levels for very large companies, but still requires further investigation to explain why this is the case.

Staffing levels for professionals and support personnel by industry group are given in Tables A-13 and A-14. The benchmarking studies by CAPS already provide much detailed staffing information.

One interesting comparison is that for manufacturing organizations versus service organizations, as shown below:

	Manufacturing	Services
Professional Staffing Average	93	72
Support Personnel Staffing Average	66	26
Ratio of Support Staff to Professional Staff	.71	.36

Clearly, service organizations tend to use significantly fewer professional and support staff compared to manufacturing organizations on the whole, and the ratio of service support staff to professional staff is about half the ratio in manufacturing.

TABLE 10
AVERAGE NUMBER OF PURCHASING PERSONNEL

Category	Head Office	Elsewhere Within the Country	Elsewhere Outside the Country	Total
Professional Purchasing Personnel				
Under $500 million	8	8	6	11
$0.5 billion to $1 billion	16	9	8	22
$1.1 billion to $5 billion	24	28	30	52
$5.1 billion to $10 billion	57	93	70	150
$10.1 billion and over	105	186	116	289
Total	**36**	**61**	**49**	**89**
Support Staff				
Under $500 million	4	5	3	6
$0.5 billion to $1 billion	7	7	5	12
$1.1 billion to $5 billion	10	19	14	27
$5.1 billion to $10 billion	16	45	39	62
$10.1 billion and over	52	259	48	251
Total	**15**	**62**	**23**	**58**

Changes in Size of Purchasing Organization

A special addition to the 1995 study was the attempt to establish information on staffing-level changes in the recent past and expectations for the coming year. It was no great surprise to see that since 1988 major downsizing of staffing levels had occurred across the board. Whether that downsizing was continuing and whether the trend was slowing was considered useful information. Table 11 indicates staffing experience over the past 12 months and best estimates for the following 12 months.

In the past 12 months only 15 percent of the respondents increased their purchasing staff while 41 percent decreased, showing the downsizing had not yet been completed. With 22 percent of the respondents downsizing by 8 percent to 10 percent and another 38 percent downsizing by at least 18 percent, substantial cuts were made in many purchasing staffs. In 44 percent of the organizations, purchasing staff levels remained the same. With the increased responsibilities identified in Tables 9 and A-4, it is evident that purchasing departments are expected to do more work with fewer people.

The expectations for the next 12 months show quite a different pattern. While 58 percent of the organizations expect to remain at current levels, 18 percent expect to increase, and 24 percent expect to downsize further. The amount of downsizing expected is much less severe than the previous 12 months, with 76 percent expected to downsize by 10 percent or less. On the upsizing side, 60 percent expected increases of at least 8 percent. It certainly appears, therefore, that the amount of downsizing is slowing and that some leveling off in staffing is taking place.

PURCHASING'S ROLE/RESPONSIBILITY/ INVOLVEMENT IN MAJOR CORPORATE ACTIVITIES

Much of the current strategic purchasing literature proposes that purchasing should have a significant role to play in major corporate initiatives not specifically geared to supply. In this 1995 research an attempt was made to see if such purchasing involvement was actually taking place and whether changes were expected over the next year.

Tables A-15 and 12 provide an overview of the results. As the summary in Table 12 confirms, outsourcing is the one corporate activity in which purchasing's current role/responsibility/involvement is somewhat above moderate and is expected to increase significantly. Yet outsourcing should by rights be an activity with major purchasing involvement. That in many outsourcing decisions purchasing is not involved at all, or barely involved, already has been confirmed in other research. The information systems area is a good example of a corporate function exposed to considerable outsourcing, without significant purchasing involvement. The 1995 CAPS study on nontraditional pur-

TABLE 11
CHANGES IN SIZE OF PURCHASING ORGANIZATION IN PAST 12 MONTHS, AND EXPECTED IN NEXT 12 MONTHS

	Past 12 Months		Next 12 Months	
	#	%	#	%
Remain Same	127	44	167	58
Upsized	43	15	51	18
0-2%	0	0	5	10
2.1-4%	4	9	2	4
4.1-6%	6	14	13	26
6.1-8%	2	5	1	2
8.1-10%	14	33	12	24
10.1-12%	1	2	1	2
12.1-14%	0	0	0	0
14.1-16%	5	12	7	14
16.1-18%	2	4	0	0
18.1-20%	5	12	3	6
20.1% and Over	4	9	7	14
Downsized	117	41	68	24
0-2%	2	2	1	2
2.1-4%	6	5	4	6
4.1-6%	15	13	22	32
6.1-8%	7	6	3	5
8.1-10%	26	22	21	31
10.1-12%	1	0	0	0
12.1-14%	2	2	1	1
14.1-16%	10	8	3	4
16.1-18%	3	3	0	0
18.1-20%	20	17	6	9
20.1% and Over	25	21	7	10
Total	287	100	286	100

chases also has confirmed the lack of purchasing involvement in many areas of corporate procurement.[4]

Purchasing's involvement in other corporate activities such as governmental relations, countertrade, marketing planning, and corporate mergers and alliances is light. Other corporate activities, such as information systems planning, corporate strategic planning, new product development, risk management, financial and technology planning, ranked low in terms of current purchasing involvement. The obvious conclusion is that purchasing still has a significant way to go before it is meaningfully involved in major corporate activities.

The predicted change index showed significant increases in terms of expectations of future involvement of purchasing in corporate activities. In all cases, purchasing's involvement was predicted to increase. Whether this represents wishful thinking, time will tell, but, at least, awareness of the challenge exists. The one notable exception is the area of governmental relations where not much change is expected.

COMMUNICATION MEANS BETWEEN HEAD OFFICE AND PURCHASING GROUPS LOCATED ELSEWHERE IN THE ORGANIZATION

How do purchasing groups geographically separated from one another within the same organization communicate with one another? In this study we focused on the communication media between head office staffs and other purchasing groups in the same company. Table 13 shows that the telephone is a clear first, with a ranking of 4.3 on a 5-point scale, followed by fax at 4.02 and e-mail at 3.71. Personal meetings at 3.03 and teleconferencing at 2.98 are moderately used, followed by letters at 2.8. Videoconferencing (2.03) is only slightly used at this time. The fairly prominent position of fax and e-mail confirms their popularity. Of those reporting extensive use, only the telephone with 40 percent, fax at 32 percent and e-mail at 40 percent were mentioned with any frequency at all; all other options showed extensive use at 7 percent or lower.

CORPORATE HEADQUARTERS' ROLE/ RESPONSIBILITY/ INVOLVEMENT IN SELECTED ACTIVITIES

What procurement-related activities are the responsibility of headquarters purchasing groups? Tables A-16 and 14 represent the range of supply-management activities and the degree of headquarters involvement in each. Table 14 provides a ranking from 1 to 15 based on an involvement index and also shows what changes are predicted over the next 12 months.

The listing of these activities confirms the more commonly assigned roles to headquarters groups and shows the prominence of policies and procedures' establishment and contracting for common requirements. The involvement of the headquarters purchasing organization in each of the activities was predicted to increase over the next 12 months. If the expected increases in headquarters involvement do materialize, the relative rankings of these might change.

---

[4] Harold E.Fearon and William A. Bales, *Purchasing of Nontraditional Goods and Services* (Tempe, AZ: Center for Advanced Purchasing Studies), 1995, 73 pages.

TABLE 12
RANKING OF PURCHASING'S CURRENT ROLE/RESPONSIBILITY/INVOLVEMENT IN MAJOR CORPORATE ACTIVITIES, AND PREDICTED CHANGE OVER NEXT 12 MONTHS

Rank	Activity	Involvement Index*	Predicted Change Index**
1	Outsourcing	3.40	+50
2	Information Systems Planning	2.89	+38
3	Capital Project/Investment Planning	2.82	+27
4	Corporate Strategic Planning	2.76	+39
5	New Product Development	2.75	+34
6	Risk Management/Hedging	2.65	+22
7	Financial/Cash Flow Planning	2.53	+28
8	Technology Planning	2.47	+25
9	Environmental Planning	2.40	+20
10	Government Relations	2.13	+ 5
11	International Countertrade/Offset Planning	2.09	+18
12	Marketing Planning	2.05	+22
13	Corporate Mergers/Acquisitions/Allilances	2.05	+17

*Involvement Index: 1 = None, 2 = Slight, 3 = Moderate, 4 = Substantial, 5 = Extensive

**Predicted Change Index: % increase minus % decrease

TABLE 13
USE OF COMMUNICATION MEDIA BETWEEN HEAD OFFICE PURCHASING AND PURCHASERS LOCATED ELSEWHERE IN THE ORGANIZATION

	Relative Use Index	# of Responses	Number and Percent of Firms Using									
			None		Slight		Moderate		Substantial		Extensive	
			#	%	#	%	#	%	#	%	#	%
Telephone	4.3	260	1	0	2	0	32	12	112	43	113	44
Fax	4.02	260	2	0	12	5	45	17	118	45	83	32
E-Mail	3.71	259	31	12	17	7	50	19	57	22	104	40
Personal meeting	3.03	255	4	2	54	21	135	53	52	20	10	4
Teleconference	2.98	247	18	7	67	27	82	33	65	27	15	6
Letter	2.8	252	17	7	88	35	90	36	38	15	19	7
Videoconference	2.03	244	84	35	88	36	54	22	13	5	5	2

(Relative Use Ranking: 1 = None, 2 = Slight, 3 = Moderate, 4 = Substantial, 5 = Extensive)

TABLE 14
**RANKING OF CURRENT ROLE/RESPONSIBILITY/INVOLVEMENT OF
CORPORATE HEADQUARTERS PURCHASING ORGANIZATION IN
SELECTED ACTIVITIES, AND PREDICTED CHANGE OVER NEXT 12 MONTHS**

Rank	Activity	Involvement Index*	Predicted Change Index**
1	Establishes policies and procedures	4.31	+19
2	Contracts for common requirements	4.12	+32
3	Purchases head offices requirements	4.00	+12
4	Collects and provides purchasing information	3.95	+33
5	Participates in system-wide purchasing/supply personnel decisions/actions	3.94	+31
6	Develops supply systems, e.g., EDI, credit cards	3.89	+51
7	Provides input to and support services for special corporate initiatives in areas such as quality, cost, timelines, productivity, customer satisfaction	3.56	+31
8	Develops and/or provides training	3.54	+30
9	Interfaces with industry/professional groups/associations	3.37	+15
10	Performs special studies and provides reports	3.35	+21
11	Measures internal customer satisfaction	3.26	+38
12	Measures supplier satisfaction	3.11	+33
13	Evaluates/audits unit/divisional performance	3.00	+21
14	Participates in interplant purchases and/or goods or services transfers	2.92	+ 9
15	Interfaces with government	2.31	+ 3

*Involvement Index: 1 = None, 2 = Slight, 3 = Moderate, 4 = Substantial, 5 = Extensive
**Predicted Change Index: % increase minus % decrease

PURCHASING'S USE OF VARIOUS PURCHASING TECHNIQUES

In recent years, much has been made of various participative approaches to increase purchasing effectiveness. Most of these approaches involve councils or teams with customers or suppliers. Tables A-17 and 15 establish just how extensive the use of such activities really is and what changes are expected over the next 12 months.

The predicted change index shows use of all of the techniques/approaches/activities is expected to increase, with the lowest predicted change index increase (24) attributed to purchasing councils; the highest were teams involving suppliers (57) and cross-functional teams (54). On the whole, participative approaches can be expected to increase in the future according to these data.

TABLE 15
**RANKING OF PURCHASING'S USE OF VARIOUS PURCHASING
TECHNIQUES/APPROACHES/ACTIVITIES, AND EXPECTED USE OVER NEXT 12 MONTHS**

Rank	Technique/Approach/Activity	Involvement Index*	Predicted Change Index**
1	Cross-functional teams	3.58	+54
2	Commodity Teams (purchasing personnel only)	3.12	+32
3	Purchasing Councils (purchasing managers only)	2.86	+24
4	Teams involving supplier(s)	2.85	+57
5	Teams involving customer(s)	2.55	+42
6	Co-location of purchasing personnel with users/specifiers	2.51	+25
7	Suppliers Councils (primarily key suppliers)	2.32	+38
8	Teams involving both supplier(s) and customer(s)	2.13	+42
9	Consortium buying (pooling with other firms)	1.49	+33

*Involvement Index: 1 = None, 2 = Slight, 3 = Moderate, 4 = Substantial, 5 = Extensive
**Predicted Change Index: % increase minus % decrease

THE CHIEF PURCHASING OFFICER (CPO)

The executive in charge of the purchasing function for an organization carries a significant load. This research, as was done in the previous study, asked a number of questions about the chief purchasing officer (CPO) with respect to title, age, educational background, and experience. On the assertion that the function can be no better than its leader, the characteristics of this person become an integral part of supply success.

Title

The titles carried by the chief purchasing officer (CPO) vary greatly from organization to organization, and a given title is not used with consistent meaning in various organizations. The duties of a person with the title of Manager of Purchasing may be similar to another person titled Vice President of Purchasing and perhaps may encompass even greater authority and responsibility. However, title does convey a degree of status.

The most commonly used title in the U.S. for the CPO are: Director of Purchasing (21%), VP of Purchasing (19%), and Manager of Purchasing (13%). In Canada, the most commonly used titles are Director of Purchasing (32%) and Manager of Purchasing (23%). Comparison with the data from 1988 shows a significant decline in popularity of the Director of Purchasing title (from 38% in 1988) as shown in Table 16.

The real surprise in this 1995 study came from the "Other" category. About 31 percent of all the respondents had a title different from those suggested in the survey, whereas in 1988 only 5 percent had different titles. Of the 95 respondents in the "Other" category, about 42 percent carried a VP title, including VP Corporate Procurement, VP Strategic Sourcing, VP Supplier Management and Procurement, and VP Purchasing and Transportation. If these VP titles were combined with the VP of Purchasing choice provided in the questionnaire, it would make the VP designation the most common one at 31 percent versus the 18 percent reported in Table 16.

The title "Director" was the next-most-common designation in the "Other" category, occurring about 25 percent of the time. Titles included: Director of Procurement; Director, Supply Chain Management; Group Director, Commercial Services Management; and Director, Logistics and Supply Management. If these Director designations were included in the Director of Purchasing category reported in Table 16, it would bring the percentage of Director designations up to 30 percent

Manager designations in the "Other" category were mentioned about 12 percent of the time and would have increased the Manager category to 18 percent. The title General Manager appeared 6 percent of the time, such as General Manager, Purchasing.

The listing of alternative titles for CPOs in Table 16 provides a wide range of choices for those aspiring to escape the traditional appellations. It shows a wide proliferation of titles, most of which have been coined in the last eight years. To no one's great surprise, the term "Purchasing Agent" is no longer used to designate the CPO in any of the companies surveyed. An adjusted ranking of titles using only the terms VP, Director, and Manager, including the data from the "Other" category shows the following: VP — 37 percent; Director — 36 percent; and Manager — 21 percent.

In Table 17, the titles of the CPO are listed by company size, showing the decline of the Manager title from 37 percent for smaller companies to 5 percent in the largest ones. The Director of Purchasing title appears most popular in companies $1.1-billion to $5-billion in size. VP Purchasing is most commonly used in the $5.1-billion to $10-billion category and, allowing for the "Other" category, a VP designation appears to be the most common one in the over $10-billion category.

In Table A-18, the titles are listed by industry group, showing significant variation between industries, but, in the aggregate, not much difference between manufacturing and service firms. For the companies that participated in both the 1995 and 1988 studies, the interesting finding in Table 18 is that 59 percent of the CPO designations were changed and that only 41 percent remained the same.

Age of the Chief Purchasing Officer

The CPO has an average age of 50. The variation in averages for different company size categories has narrowed somewhat since 1988. In 1988, the average age of CPOs in companies under $500 million in sales was just below 47 years, whereas it became 50 years in 1995. The average age for CPOs working in companies in the $500-million to $1-billion group was 49 and for those working for companies over $10 billion in size it was 51. All others averaged 50 years and the total group average was 50 years. The percentage distribution of ages in each company size range stayed approximately the same as in 1988. Table 19 provides the age profiles for the 299 respondents to this question.

Table A-19 provides age profiles across industries showing a remarkable consistency for the averages of manufacturing and service organizations. For manufacturing industries with a significant number of respondents, aerospace had 70 percent of CPOs age 51 and over, food and beverage 65 percent age 50 and under, and paper 61 percent age 50 and under.

TABLE 16
TITLE OF CHIEF PURCHASING OFFICER (CPO), FOR
1995 STUDY (U.S., CANADA, AND TOTAL) AND 1988 STUDY
NUMBER OF ORGANIZATIONS, AND PERCENT

Title of CPO	1995 Study						1988 Study	
	U.S.		Canada		Total			
	#	%	#	%	#	%	#	%
Purchasing Agent	0	0	0	0	0	0	2	1
Manager of Purchasing	35	13	7	23	42	14	52	18
Director of Purchasing	58	21	10	32	68	22	112	38
VP of Purchasing	52	19	1	3	53	18	67	22
Materials Manager	8	3	2	6	10	3	6	2
Director of Materials	20	7	0	0	20	6	16	5
VP of Materials Management	20	7	0	0	20	6	26	9
Other	84*	30	11**	36	95	31	16	5
Total	277	100	31	100	308	100	297	100

* The other titles were: VP, Energy & Materials; General Manager, Purchasing and Transportation; VP Materials; General Manager of Materials and Services; VP Logistics; Manager - Contract Administration; VP/General Manager Supplier Management; VP Sourcing; Materials & Services Manager; VP - Procurement; Executive Director of Procurement; VP of Corporate Supply Management; Director of Central Procurement; Assistant VP; Manager of Corporate Procurement & Materials Management; Senior VP Materials Management; VP Purchasing & Package Engineering; General Manager, Purchasing; Corporate VP & Director of Supply & Environmental Management; General Manager - Corporate Purchasing; VP Subcontracts & Procurement (Corporate); VP, Purchasing and Distribution and VP Controller - Worldside Industrial; Senior Purchasing Manager; Manager of Procurement & Material Control; VP of Strategic Sourcing; Director of Corporate Transportation & Purchasing; Corporate Director of Procurement; Executive Director; Director Supply Chain Management; Manager, Procurement and Materials Management; Assistant General Manager; VP Corporate Services; VP Corporate Procurement; Executive Director, Global Procurement; Director Contracts and Purchasing; VP Equipment & Purchasing; VP Procurement and Support Services; Director - Materials & Services; Director - Supply Management; Senior VP and Chief Procurement Officer; VP Director Corporate Procurement; Assistant VP - Procurement Services; VP Worldwide Procurement; Director of Materials &Logistics; VP Purchasing & Materials Control; Group Director, Commercial Services Management; Manager of Corporate Procurement and Materials Management; VP Supplier Management and Procurement; First VP and Director, Sourcing; Managing Director; VP Strategic Sourcing; VP Purchasing & Transportation; Director of Materials Management; Manager of Procurement & Materials Management; Manager of Procurement and Director of Purchasing; Director of Procurement; Director - Financial Services; VP Supply & Services; Assistnt VP of Purcasing & Materials Management; Assistant VP - Purchasing; Assistant VP Materials Management; VP of purchasing & Distribution; Director Strategic Procurement; VP, Purchasing and Logistics; VP - Administration; General Manager, Materials and Logistics; VP - Purchasing, Transportation & Energy; VP, Supply Management; VP Purchasing, Transportation & Properties; Director - Purchaisng & Logistics; VP Procurement; Vice President - Supply Process; GM Sourcing; Executive Director, Purchasing; VP, Director of Central Purchasing & Packaging; Manager Procurement; Vp Purchasing and QA; Director of purchasing and Transportation.

** The other Canadian titles were: Manager, Supply Management; VP - Logistics (Acquisition, Distribution & Fleet); Director, Supply Management; Manager, Materials and Services Supply; Chief of Supply Management; Director of Procurement; Director, Procurement; General Manager; VP Purchases & Materials; VP Global Operations Planning; Director, Logistics & Supply Management.

TABLE 17
TITLE OF CHIEF PURCHASING OFFICER, BY COMPANY SIZE

Title	1994 Sales Revenue											
	Under $500 million		$0.5 billion to $1 billion		$1.1 billion to $5 billion		$5.1 bilion to $10 billion		$10.1 billion and over		Total	
	#	%	#	%	#	%	#	%	#	%	#	%
Manager of Purchasing	16	37	11	20	9	8	4	9	2	5	42	14
Director of Purchasing	8	19	10	19	37	32	9	19	3	7	67	22
VP of Purchasing	5	12	7	13	19	16	13	28	9	20	53	17
Materials Manager	1	2	4	7	4	3	0	0	0	0	9	3
Director of Material	5	12	8	15	5	4	1	2	0	0	19	6
VP of Materials Management	3	7	1	2	8	7	2	4	6	14	20	7
Other	5	12	13	24	35	30	18	38	24	55	95	31
Total*	43	101	54	100	117	100	47	100	44	101	305	100

*Totals may not add up to 100 due to rounding.

TABLE 18
CHANGE IN TITLE OF THE CHIEF PURCHASING OFFICER BETWEEN 1988 AND 1995
(SAME 118 COMPANIES)

Title of the CPO (1988 versus 1995)	#	%
Total Number of Respondents	118	100
Number in Which Title Remained the Same	48	41
Number in Which Title Changed	70	59

TABLE 19
AGE OF THE CHIEF PURCHASING OFFICER, BY COMPANY SIZE

Age of CPO	1994 Sales Revenue																	
	Under $500 million			$0.5 billion to $1 billion			$1.1 billion to $5 billion			$5.1 billion to $10 billion			$10.1 billion and over			Total		
	#	%	Average	#	%	Average	#	%	Average	#	%	Average	#	%	Average	#	%	Average
30-40	5	12	37	7	13	38	11	9	37	6	13	38	5	12	39	34	11	38
41-50	14	33	46	24	44	47	46	40	46	17	38	47	12	29	47	113	38	47
51-60	19	45	54	22	41	55	54	47	54	20	44	54	22	52	55	137	46	54
61 and Over	4	10	62	1	2	70	5	4	63	2	4	64	3	7	62	15	5	63
Total*	42	100	50	54	100	49	116	100	50	45	99	50	42	100	51	299	100	50

*Totals may not add up to 100 due to rounding.

CPO's Educational Background

CPOs of large organizations are well educated. On the U.S. side, 56 percent had a bachelor's degree and another 40 percent a graduate degree, indicating that 96 percent were college graduates. On the Canadian side, 58 percent had a bachelor's degree and 19 percent an advanced degree, totaling 77 percent as university graduates. The 1995 results were almost the same as the 1988 findings as is shown in Table 20.

Table 21 shows the educational profile of the CPO by company size. It shows that the bigger the company, the greater becomes the percentage of CPOs holding an advanced degree. In companies under $500 million in sales size, 18 percent held advanced degrees versus 57 percent in companies over $10 billion. As might be expected, those who hold only high school diplomas dropped steadily from 19 percent for companies under $500 million in sales to none in the largest companies.

A business degree (58%) is the most-common bachelor's degree held as shown in Table 22. This is followed by Engineering (19%), and Liberal Arts (12%). These figures are almost identical to those of 1988.

The industry breakdown in Table A-20 shows few significant variations within the manufacturing group. When the manufacturing average is compared to the service average, some interesting differences emerge:

EDUCATION OF CPO

	High School		Bachelor's Degree		Advanced Degree	
	1995 %	1988 %	1995 %	1988 %	1995 %	1988 %
Manufacturing	6	7	53	56	41	38
Service	3	7	67	45	30	48

Since 1988, when the services area showed the highest level of advanced degree holders at 48 percent, this number slipped to 30 percent in 1995, whereas manufacturing increased over the same period from 38 percent to 41 percent.

TABLE 20
EDUCATION OF CHIEF PURCHASING OFFICER,
1995 STUDY (U.S., CANADA, AND TOTAL)
AND 1988 STUDY

Highest Education	1995 Study						1988 Study	
	U.S.		Canada		Total			
	#	%	#	%	#	%	#	%
High School	10	4	7	23	17	5	19	6
Bachelor's Degree	154	56	18	58	170	56	161	55
Graduate Degree	113	40	6	19	118	39	115	39
Total	277	100	31	100	305	100	295	100

TABLE 21
EDUCATION OF CHIEF PURCHASING OFFICER, BY ORGANIZATION SIZE

Highest Education Level	1995 Study 1994 Sales Revenue												1988 Study	
	Under $500 million		$0.5 billion to $1 billion		$1.1 billion $5 billion		$5.1 billion to $10 billion		$10.1 billion and over		Total		Total	
	#	%	#	%	#	%	#	%	#	%	#	%	#	%
High School	8	19	4	7	4	3	1	2	0	0	17	5	19	6
Bachelor's Degree	27	63	34	63	64	55	26	55	19	43	170	56	161	55
Graduate Degree	8	18	16	30	49	42	20	43	25	57	118	39	115	39
Total	43	100	54	100	117	100	47	100	44	100	305	100	295	100

TABLE 22
SPECIALIZATION IN BACHELOR'S DEGREE WORK, BY ORGANIZATION SIZE

Functional Area	(1994 Sales Revenue)												(1986 Sales Revenue)	
	Under $500 million		$0.5 billion to $1 billion		$1.1 billion $5 billion		$5.1 billion to $10 billion		$10.1 billion and over		Total			
	#	%	#	%	#	%	#	%	#	%	#	%	#	%
Business	16	59	19	56	38	59	14	56	11	58	98	58	147	55
Engineering	3	11	5	15	14	22	6	24	4	21	32	19	50	19
Liberal Arts	2	8	4	12	10	16	4	16	1	5	21	12	34	13
Other	6	22	6	17	2	3	1	4	3	16	18	11	35	13
Total	**27**	**100**	**34**	**100**	**64**	**100**	**25**	**100**	**19**	**100**	**169**	**100**	**266**	**100**

Table A-21 shows academic specialization on the bachelor's degree by industry group. The differences between the manufacturing and service sectors are noteworthy as the following summary shows:

Industry Segment	Business		Engineering		Liberal Arts		Other	
	1995 %	1988 %	1995 %	1988 %	1995 %	1988 %	1995 %	1988 %
Manufacturing	53	53	22	20	11	13	14	13
Service	70	68	11	8	15	12	4	12

Graduate Degrees

The most-common graduate degree held by CPOs is an MBA (70%). Advanced degrees in management, other than an MBA, amounted to another 12 percent. Six percent had a Ph.D., 5 percent a graduate engineering degree, 4 percent an economics master's and 3 percent multiple master's degrees like an MBA and MS Engineering, and 2 percent had a law degree. Comparable detailed data were not collected in 1988.

CPO's Years in Present Position

Table 23 provides an overview of the years the current CPO has spent in this position. The majority (61%) has been in the current position for five years or less, although the company size ranges show significant variation, with a low of 48 percent of those working in the below $500-million size companies and a high of 79 percent in the $5.1-billion to $10-billion range. The comparison with the 1988 study shows that most distributions are reasonably similar with the exception of the over $10-billion group, where in the previous study 85 percent had been in the 5 years or less category compared to 69 percent for the 1995 group.

TABLE 23
THE CHIEF PURCHASING OFFICER: YEARS IN PRESENT POSITION, BY ORGANIZATION SIZE

Years in Present Position	(1994 Sales Revenue)											
	Under $500 million		$0.5 billion to $1 billion		$1.1 billion to $5 billion		$5.1 billion to $10 billion		$10.1 billion and over		Total	
	#	%	#	%	#	%	#	%	#	%	#	%
1-5 Years	20	48	31	58	67	58	37	79	29	69	184	61
6-10 Years	11	26	13	24	31	26	5	11	11	26	71	23
11-15 Years	6	14	6	11	13	11	3	6	2	5	30	10
Over 15 Years	5	12	4	7	6	5	2	4	0	0	17	6
Total	42	100	54	100	117	100	47	100	42	100	302	100
Average Years	8.0		6.5		6.2		4.2		4.3		5.9	

The average years on the job for each CPO see a peak of 8.0 years for firms in smaller companies to lows of 4.2 and 4.3 years for firms in the largest size range. The 1988 comparison shows that these figures have not changed much.

The industry group comparison in Table A-22 shows that manufacturing firms have 7 percent of the respondents in the over 15 years in the present position category, whereas the services group had none. On the other hand, services had 17 percent of all respondents in the 11- to 15-years group compared with 8 percent for manufacturing. For 10 or fewer years, both groups had almost identical results with about 60 percent in the 1- to 5-year range and 24 percent in the 6- to 10-year range.

CPO's Years with Present Employer

Table 24 shows the number of years the current CPO has worked for the present employer. The largest number clearly fell into the over 15-year category. Comparison with the 1988 study shows that in the over $10-billion-sales category 16 percent have five years' experience or fewer with their current employer in 1995, while in 1988 the corresponding number was 4 percent. This shows that more large companies in the last few years were willing to bring in outsiders for the CPO position than they were earlier.

TABLE 24
THE CHIEF PURCHASING OFFICER: YEARS WITH PRESENT EMPLOYER, BY ORGANIZATION SIZE

Years with Present Employer	(1994 Sales Revenue)											
	Under $500 million		$0.5 billion to $1 billion		$1.1 billion to $5 billion		$5.1 billion to $10 billion		$10.1 billion and over		Total	
	#	%	#	%	#	%	#	%	#	%	#	%
1-5 Years	8	19	7	13	15	13	5	11	7	16	42	14
6-10 Years	4	9	9	17	20	17	6	13	5	11	44	15
11-15 Years	6	14	9	17	19	16	3	6	4	9	41	13
Over 15 Years	25	58	29	53	62	54	33	70	28	64	177	58
Total	43	100	54	100	116	100	47	100	44	100	304	100
Average Years	18.2		16.8		17.7		19.3		21.1		18.3	

The industry group comparison for the CPO's years with present employer data is shown in Table A-23. Although some variations do exist between industries, for those with larger numbers of participating companies, the data are reasonably similar as they are for the total manufacturing versus services comparison:

	1-5 years %	6-10 years %	11-15 years %	Over 15 years %	Average years
Manufacturing	12	15	14	59	18.5
Service	19	13	11	57	17.8

The comparison of average years with present employers shows that the highest number (21.1 years) occurs in the largest companies, and the lowest number (16.8 years) occurs in the $0.5-billion to $1-billion size range. In 1988 these figures were reasonably similar.

CPO's Years Experience in All Functional Areas

Table 25 shows the CPO's years of experience in all functional areas, with all present and past employers, by categories of size of organization. The summary below provides the information on CPO's average years experience for both 1995 and 1988 in descending order.

Thus, although the number of years of purchasing experience has decreased slightly from 17.0 years to

CPO's YEARS EXPERIENCE IN:

	1995	1988
Purchasing	16.3	17.0
Operations/Production	4.6	4.0
Other	2.1	0.7
MIS	1.0	0.5
Engineering	0.9	1.3
Accounting	0.9	0.6
Marketing	0.8	1.6
Finance	0.7	0.8
Traffic/Distribution/Logistics	0.3	1.0

TABLE 25

THE CHIEF PURCHASING OFFICER : AVERAGE YEARS' EXPERIENCE IN ALL FUNCTIONAL AREAS, BY ORGANIZATION SIZE

Functional Area	Sales Revenue					
	Under $5 million	$0.5 billion to $1 billion	$1.1 billion to $5 billion	$5.1 billion to $10 billion	$10.1 billion and over	Total
Purchasing	22.7	16.8	15.6	12.4	15.0	16.3
Operations/Production	2.2	4.0	3.9	6.1	8.2	4.6
Engineering	0.1	0.7	0.9	2.1	0.9	0.9
Marketing	0.2	0.6	1.1	0.6	1.0	0.8
Accounting	0.0	0.8	0.9	1.4	1.0	0.9
Traffic/Distribution/Logistics	0.0	0.8	0.3	0.2	0.3	0.3
MIS	0.5	0.9	1.3	0.9	1.2	1.0
Finance	0.9	0.4	0.8	0.5	0.5	0.7
Other	1.1	3.0	2.3	3.1	0.5	2.1
Total Responses	**42**	**53**	**114**	**43**	**42**	**294**

16.3 years, the change in experience in other functional areas is interesting. Clearly, many current CPOs have significant experience outside of the procurement area. Operations and production at 4.6 years outpaces the other functional areas. MIS experience is up significantly from the earlier study, having moved from last place to fourth place. Traffic/distribution/logistics dropped significantly from fifth place in 1988 to last place in 1995. Marketing also moved substantially from third ranking to seventh.

The industry comparison shown in Table A-24 shows some significant variations between industries as to the CPO's experience in different functional areas. The manufacturing versus service comparison for both 1995 and 1988 is shown below.

CPO's YEARS EXPERIENCE IN:

	Manufacturing		Service	
	1995	1988	1995	1988
Purchasing	16.3	17.0	16.3	15.0
Operations/Production	4.5	4.0	4.7	4.6
Other	2.0	0.7	3.2	0.5
MIS	1.1	0.6	0.8	0.0
Engineering	1.0	1.3	0.6	1.8
Accounting	0.8	0.6	0.8	0.2
Marketing	0.9	1.6	0.6	1.0
Finance	0.7	0.8	0.7	0.3
Traffic/Distribution/ Logistics	0.3	1.0	0.4	0.0

This summary shows that the additional experience for CPOs in services has changed about the same as in the manufacturing sector. In the services area, the number of years in "Other," at 3.2, is significantly higher than the 2.0 years for manufacturing CPOs. Manufacturing CPOs tend to have more MIS, engineering, and marketing experience, however.

MAJOR INNOVATIONS/CHANGES BY 2001

An open-ended question at the end of the questionnaire asked the respondents to indicate what major purchasing changes they believed would contribute significantly to their organization by 2001. A total of 232 replies were received, ranging from one-word answers to small essays. A ranking of the most frequently mentioned changes (Table 26) shows systems changes (47%) far ahead of any other category.

Interesting comments included the following seven replies:

1. We do not have to be "new or creative." We need to mind our ABCs. Buy where it makes sense; partner; reduce supply base; work jointly with suppliers to reduce costs; etc., etc., all standard stuff!

2. Distributed use of purchasing talent/processes via hundreds of teams networked globally through technology; a dynamic breathing organization, which is very nimble.

3. Direct line reporting from (nonpurchasing department) satellite purchasing employers.

4. Evolution from transaction-based/focused buyers to client-oriented consultants setting up mecha-

TABLE 26

MAJOR INNOVATIONS / CHANGES EXPECTED IN PURCHASING BY 2001

Change	Frequency of Mention %
Integrated systems, EDI, etc.	47
Strategic Orientation to Procurement/Sourcing	9
Supplier Partnerships / Alliances	9
Cross-Functional Teams	9
Upgrading /Training of Staff	7
Global Teaming	6
Outsourcing	6
Reporting Line Changes/Titles	6
Centralization (more)	5
Procurement Cards	5
Improved Communication	5
Focus on Value-Added Activities	4
Supply-Chain Management	4
Supplier Base Reduction	3
Decentralization (more)	3
Reengineering	3
Total Cost of Ownership Focus	3
Involvement in Nontraditional Purchases	2
Supplier Consignment of Inventory	2
Consortium Buying	1

nisms for clients to acquire directly what they need in the most cost-effective manner.

5. Become "leaner and meaner"— after all, "anyone can buy."

6. Facilitating a collaborative design process between our key suppliers and our design engineering.

7. Full use of commodity, self-managed teams for goods and services, matrixed to clients and commodity specialties, supplemented with fully functional integrated computer systems linking planning, operations, maintenance, warehousing, and finance. Accounts payable will be part of the purchasing function, but downsized with technology and process improvement.

Clear separation of transaction processing activities from professional sourcing; this latter group will be composed of well-educated staff with diverse background experiences who will become managers of processes and continually initate cost-reduction opportunities.

Table A-25 provides an overview of the responses for each of the major questions, arranged by industry group.

APPENDIX A •

TABLES A-1 THROUGH A-25

TABLE A-1
RESPONDING ORGANIZATIONS, BY INDUSTRY GROUP AND SIZE

Industry Group	1994 Sales Revenue											
	Under $500 million		$0.5 billion to $1 billion		$1.1 billion to $5 billion		$5.1 billion to $10 billion		$10.1 billion and over		Total	
	#	%	#	%	#	%	#	%	#	%	#	%
Aerospace	7	25	5	19	7	26	4	15	4	15	27	100
Apparel	1	25	2	50	1	25	0	0	0	0	4	100
Chemicals	4	12	4	13	13	42	7	23	3	10	31	100
Electronics	10	20	7	13	18	35	7	14	9	18	51	100
Fabricated Metal	1	33	0	0	1	33	1	34	0	0	3	100
Food and Beverage	1	4	6	26	10	44	6	26	0	0	23	100
Furniture and Fixtures	1	100	0	0	0	0	0	0	0	0	1	100
Instruments, related products	1	50	0	0	1	50	0	0	0	0	2	100
Lumber and Wood	0	0	1	25	3	75	0	0	0	0	4	100
Machinery except Electrical	2	50	1	25	1	25	0	0	0	0	4	100
Miscellaneous Manufacturing	5	72	0	0	0	0	1	14	1	14	7	100
Paper	2	10	4	20	8	40	4	20	2	10	20	100
Petroleum and Coal	0	0	0	0	6	32	3	16	10	52	19	100
Primary Metals	3	20	4	27	6	40	2	13	0	0	15	100
Printing and Publishing	0	0	2	50	2	50	0	0	0	0	4	100
Rubber and Plastics	0	0	2	100	0	0	0	0	0	0	2	100
Stone, Clay and Glass	0	0	0	0	1	50	1	50	0	0	2	100
Textiles	0	0	2	67	1	33	0	0	0	0	3	100
Tobacco products	0	0	1	50	1	50	0	0	0	0	2	100
Transportation Equipment	0	0	0	0	8	62	2	15	3	23	13	100
MANUFACTURING TOTAL	38	16	41	17	88	37	38	16	32	14	237	100
Services	5	7	13	19	29	43	9	13	12	18	68	100
TOTAL #	**43**	**15**	**54**	**18**	**117**	**38**	**47**	**15**	**44**	**14**	**305**	**100**

TABLE A-2
CENTRALIZATION AND DECENTRALIZATION OF THE PURCHASING FUNCTION, BY INDUSTRY GROUP

Industry Name	Centralized		Centralized/ Decentralized		Decentralized		Total	
	#	%	#	%	#	%	#	%
Aerospace	4	15	15	58	7	27	26	100
Apparel	0	0	3	75	1	25	4	100
Chemicals	3	10	23	74	5	16	31	100
Electronics	3	6	42	82	6	12	51	100
Fabricated Metal	1	33	0	0	2	67	3	100
Food and Beverage	12	52	10	44	1	4	23	100
Furniture and Fixtures	0	0	1	100	0	0	1	100
Machinery, except Electrical	1	25	2	50	1	25	4	100
Instruments, related products	1	50	1	50	0	0	2	100
Lumber and Wood	0	0	1	25	3	75	4	100
Miscellaneous Manufacturing	5	71	2	29	0	0	7	100
Paper	2	10	15	75	3	15	20	100
Petroleum and Coal	5	25	14	70	1	5	20	100
Primary Metals	4	27	8	53	3	20	15	100
Printing and Publishing	1	25	3	75	0	0	4	100
Rubber and Plastics	2	100	0	0	0	0	2	100
Stone, Clay and Glass	0	0	2	100	0	0	2	100
Textiles	1	33	2	67	0	0	3	100
Tobacco Products	1	50	1	50	0	0	2	100
Transportation Equipment	2	15	9	70	2	15	13	100
MANUFACTURING TOTAL	48	20	154	65	35	15	237	100
Services	22	32	44	65	2	3	68	100
Total #*	**70**	**23**	**198**	**65**	**37**	**12**	**305**	**100**

*Totals may not add up to 100 due to rounding.

TO WHOM PURCHASING REPORTS, BY INDUSTRY GROUP

Industry Group	Title of Person to Whom Chief Purchasing Officer Reports																		
	President		Exec VP		Sr. VP/ Group VP		Admin VP		Financial VP		Mfg/ Prdn/ Ops VP		Materials/ Logistics VP		Engineer- ing VP		Other		Total	
	#	%	#	%	#	%	#	%	#	%	#	%	#	%	#	%	#	%	#	%
Aerospace	5	19	1	4	3	12	3	12	2	7	7	26	1	4	1	4	3	12	26	100
Apparel	0	0	0	0	1	25	0	0	0	0	2	50	0	0	0	0	1	25	4	100
Chemicals	3	10	5	17	3	10	4	13	0	0	4	13	5	17	0	0	6	20	30	100
Electronics	9	17	10	20	5	10	1	2	8	16	9	17	5	10	0	0	4	8	51	100
Fabricated Metal	1	33	1	34	0	0	1	33	0	0	0	0	0	0	0	0	0	0	3	100
Food and Beverage	1	5	5	23	8	36	0	0	0	0	4	18	2	9	0	0	2	9	22	100
Furniture and Fixtures	0	0	0	0	1	100	0	0	0	0	0	0	0	0	0	0	0	0	1	100
Instruments	0	0	1	50	0	0	0	0	0	0	1	50	0	0	0	0	0	0	2	100
Lumber and Wood	1	25	0	0	1	25	0	0	0	0	2	50	0	0	0	0	0	0	4	100
Machinery, except Electrical	1	25	0	0	1	25	0	0	0	0	2	50	0	0	0	0	0	0	4	100
Miscellaneous Manufacturing	1	14	0	0	3	44	0	0	1	14	1	14	0	0	0	0	1	14	7	100
Paper	4	20	2	10	5	25	1	5	2	10	2	10	3	15	0	0	1	5	20	100
Petroleum and Coal	2	10	1	5	0	0	6	30	1	5	3	15	0	0	1	5	6	30	20	100
Primary Metal	3	20	2	13	0	0	3	20	2	13	0	0	0	0	0	0	5	34	15	100
Printing and Publishing	1	25	0	0	1	25	0	0	2	50	0	0	0	0	0	0	0	0	4	100
Rubber and Plastics	0	0	0	0	1	50	0	0	0	0	0	0	1	50	0	0	0	0	2	100
Stone, Clay and Glass	0	0	2	100	0	0	0	0	0	0	0	0	0	0	0	0	0	0	2	100
Textiles	1	33	0	0	0	0	0	0	1	34	1	33	0	0	0	0	0	0	3	100
Tobacco products	1	50	1	50	0	0	0	0	0	0	0	0	0	0	0	0	0	0	2	100
Transportation Equipment	3	23	2	15	2	15	2	15	0	0	3	24	1	8	0	0	0	0	13	100
MANUFAC- TURING #	37	16	33	14	35	15	21	9	19	8	41	17	18	8	2	1	29	12	235	100
Services	8	12	14	20	22	32	5	7	8	12	3	4	2	3	0	0	7	10	69	100
Total #	45	15	47	15	57	19	26	9	27	9	44	13	20	7	2	1	36	12	304	100

TABLE A-4
FUNCTIONS THAT REPORT TO PURCHASING, BY INDUSTRY GROUP

Industry Group

Function	Aerospace		Apparel		Chemicals		Electronic		Fabricated Metal		Food		Furniture		Industrial Machinery		Instruments, Related Products		Lumber		Miscellaneous Manufacturing		Paper		Petroleum		Primary Metal		Printing		Rubber		Services		Stone		Textile		Tobacco		Transportation		Total	
	#	%	#	%	#	%	#	%	#	%	#	%	#	%	#	%	#	%	#	%	#	%	#	%	#	%	#	%	#	%	#	%	#	%	#	%	#	%	#	%	#	%	#	%
Purchasing	26	100	4	100	31	100	50	100	3	100	23	100	1	100	4	100	2	100	4	100	7	100	20	100	20	100	15	100	4	100	2	100	69	100	2	100	3	100	2	100	13	100	305	100
Production Scheduling	4	15	1	25	0	0	5	10	0	0	3	13	0	0	0	0	0	0	0	0	0	0	0	0	2	10	0	0	0	0	0	0	4	6	0	0	0	0	0	0	3	23	22	7
Material Planning	13	50	2	50	7	23	22	44	1	33	9	39	0	0	1	25	0	0	0	0	1	14	4	20	10	50	10	67	2	50	2	100	31	45	0	0	1	33	1	50	5	38	122	40
Receiving	10	38	1	25	5	16	17	34	1	33	2	9	0	0	1	25	0	0	2	50	4	57	9	45	9	45	9	60	1	25	1	50	32	46	2	100	0	0	1	50	3	23	108	35
Material & Purchasing Research	13	50	2	50	21	68	26	52	1	33	14	61	1	100	1	25	0	0	1	25	4	57	9	45	15	75	11	73	3	75	1	50	46	67	2	100	2	67	2	100	10	77	185	61
Stores/ Warehousing	9	35	1	25	8	26	19	38	1	33	3	13	1	100	1	25	0	0	3	75	4	57	12	60	13	65	10	67	1	25	1	50	32	46	0	0	1	33	1	50	5	38	126	41
Inplant Material Movement	5	19	0	0	3	10	13	26	0	0	2	9	0	0	0	0	0	0	0	0	1	14	2	10	4	20	7	47	1	25	0	0	21	30	0	0	0	0	0	0	1	8	60	20
Inbound Traffic	13	50	2	50	12	39	23	46	3	100	6	26	1	100	2	50	0	0	4	100	1	14	6	30	13	65	13	87	1	25	2	100	41	59	2	100	2	67	0	0	9	69	156	51
Outbound Traffic	12	46	2	50	9	29	19	38	2	67	1	4	0	0	2	50	0	0	0	0	1	14	5	25	9	45	11	73	1	25	1	50	34	49	2	100	1	33	0	0	7	54	119	39
Scrap, Surplus Disposal; Inventory Recovery	10	38	2	50	18	58	32	64	1	33	11	48	1	100	3	75	0	0	4	100	6	86	16	80	16	80	14	93	2	50	2	100	38	55	0	0	3	100	2	100	11	85	192	63
Quality Assurance	6	23	2	50	1	3	14	28	0	0	6	26	0	0	1	25	0	0	0	0	1	14	3	15	9	45	4	27	0	0	0	0	27	39	0	0	1	33	0	0	3	23	78	26
Inventory Control	10	38	1	25	4	13	21	42	1	33	9	39	0	0	1	25	0	0	3	75	2	29	7	35	12	60	12	80	1	25	1	50	35	51	1	50	1	33	1	50	6	46	128	42
Other	9	35	1	25	5	16	16	32	0	0	7	30	0	0	1	25	0	0	2	50	0	0	6	30	7	35	0	0	1	25	1	50	22	32	1	50	0	0	1	50	2	15	82	27

TABLE A-5
NUMBER OF PROFESSIONAL PURCHASING PERSONNEL, BY ORGANIZATION SIZE, HEAD OFFICE ONLY

Number of People	Sales Revenue											
	Under $500 million		$0.5 billion to $1 billion		$1.1 billion to $5 billion		$5.1 billion to $10 billion		$10.1 billion and over		Total	
	#	%	#	%	#	%	#	%	#	%	#	%
25 or Less	41	98	41	84	88	80	23	56	11	28	204	72
26-100	1	2	7	14	17	15	15	36	18	45	58	21
101-250	0	0	1	2	4	4	1	2	8	20	14	5
251-500	0	0	0	0	1	1	1	2	2	5	4	1
501-1000	0	0	0	0	0	0	1	2	1	2	2	1
Total	42	100	49	100	110	100	41	98	40	100	282	100

*Totals may not add up to 100 due to rounding.

TABLE A-6
NUMBER OF PROFESSIONAL PURCHASING PERSONNEL, BY ORGANIZATION SIZE, ELSEWHERE WITHIN THIS COUNTRY

Number of People	Sales Revenue											
	Under $500 million		$0.5 billion to $1 billion		$1.1 billion to $5 billion		$5.1 billion to $10 billion		$10.1 billion and over		Total	
	#	%	#	%	#	%	#	%	#	%	#	%
25 or Less	15	94	30	100	43	60	10	30	4	13	102	56
26-100	1	6	0	0	27	37	13	40	13	43	54	30
101-250	0	0	0	0	2	3	7	21	7	24	16	9
251-500	0	0	0	0	0	0	3	9	4	13	7	4
501-1000	0	0	0	0	0	0	0	0	2	7	2	1
Total	16	100	30	100	72	100	33	100	30	100	181	100

TABLE A-7
NUMBER OF PROFESSIONAL PURCHASING PERSONNEL, BY ORGANIZATION SIZE, ELSEWHERE OUTSIDE THIS COUNTRY

Number of People	Sales Revenue											
	Under $500 million		$0.5 billion to $1 billion		$1.1 billion to $5 billion		$5.1 billion to $10 billion		$10.1 billion and over		Total	
	#	%	#	%	#	%	#	%	#	%	#	%
25 or Less	6	100	12	92	26	67	5	33	4	22	53	58
26-100	0	0	1	8	10	26	6	40	8	44	25	28
101-250	0	0	0	0	3	7	4	27	5	28	12	13
251-500	0	0	0	0	0	0	0	0	1	6	1	1
Total	6	100	13	100	39	100	15	100	18	100	91	100

TABLE A-8
NUMBER OF PROFESSIONAL PURCHASING PERSONNEL, BY ORGANIZATION SIZE
TOTAL IN HEAD OFFICE AND ELSEWHERE, DOMESTIC AND INTERNATIONAL

Number of People	Sales Revenue															Total		
	Under $500 million			$0.5 billion to $1 billion			$1.1 billion $5 billion			$5.1 billion to $10 billion			$10.1 billion and over					
	#	%	Average	#	%	Average	#	%	Average	#	%	Average	#	%	Average	#	%	Average
25 or Less	39	91	8	40	77	11	43	39	14	7	16	18	3	7	13	132	45	12
26-100	4	9	43	11	21	54	56	50	46	18	42	58	9	22	71	98	33	51
101-250	0	0	-	1	2	124	8	7	135	8	19	172	14	34	179	31	11	164
251-500	0	0	-	0	0	-	4	4	376	9	21	351	6	15	348	19	7	355
501-1000	0	0	-	0	0	-	0	0	-	1	2	750	7	17	642	8	3	656
1001 and Over	0	0	-	0	0	-	0	0	-	0	0	-	2	5	1051	2	1	1051
Total #	43	100	11	52	100	22	111	100	52	43	100	150	41	100	289	290	100	89

TABLE A-9
NUMBER OF SUPPORT PURCHASING PERSONNEL, BY ORGANIZATION SIZE, HEAD OFFICE ONLY

Number of People	Sales Revenue										Total	
	Under $500 million		$0.5 billion to $1 billion		$1.1 billion to $5 billion		$5.1 billion to $10 billion		$10.1 billion and over			
	#	%	#	%	#	%	#	%	#	%	#	%
25 or Less	38	100	45	96	96	92	31	79	20	55	230	87
26-100	0	0	2	4	8	8	8	21	11	31	29	11
101-250	0	0	0	0	0	0	0	0	3	8	3	1
251-500	0	0	0	0	0	0	0	0	2	6	2	1
Total	38	100	47	100	104	100	39	100	36	100	264	100

TABLE A-10
NUMBER OF SUPPORT PURCHASING PERSONNEL, BY ORGANIZATION SIZE,
ELSEWHERE WITHIN THIS COUNTRY

Number of People	Sales Revenue										Total	
	Under $500 million		$0.5 billion to $1 billion		$1.1 billion to $5 billion		$5.1 billion to $10 billion		$10.1 billion and over			
	#	%	#	%	#	%	#	%	#	%	#	%
25 or Less	12	100	26	96	49	79	15	53	9	35	111	72
26-100	0	0	1	4	11	18	10	36	12	46	34	21
101-250	0	0	0	0	2	3	3	11	3	11	8	5
501-1000	0	0	0	0	0	0	0	0	1	4	1	1
1001 and Over	0	0	0	0	0	0	0	0	1	4	1	1
Total #	12	100	27	100	62	100	28	100	26	100	155	100

TABLE A-11
NUMBER OF SUPPORT PURCHASING PERSONNEL,
BY ORGANIZATION SIZE, ELSEWHERE OUTSIDE THIS COUNTRY

Number of People	Sales Revenue										Total	
	Under $500 million		$0.5 billion to $1 billion		$1.1 billion to $5 billion		$5.1 billion to $10 billion		$10.1 billion and over			
	#	%	#	%	#	%	#	%	#	%	#	%
25 or Less	5	100	10	100	28	88	7	54	5	38	55	75
26-100	0	0	0	0	3	9	5	38	7	54	15	21
101-250	0	0	0	0	1	3	1	8	1	8	3	4
Total #	5	100	10	100	32	100	13	100	13	100	73	100

TABLE A-12
NUMBER OF SUPPORT PURCHASING PERSONNEL, BY ORGANIZATION SIZE,
TOTAL IN HEAD OFFICE AND ELSEWHERE, DOMESTIC AND INTERNATIONAL

Number of People	Sales Revenue															Total		
	Under $500 million			$0.5 billion to $1 billion			$1.1 billion to $5 billion			$5.1 billion to $10 billion			$10.1 billion and over					
	#	%	Average	#	%	Average	#	%	Average	#	%	Average	#	%	Average	#	%	Average
25 or Less	39	100	6	44	90	8	75	71	10	16	41	11	6	15	12	180	67	9
26-100	0	0	-	5	10	45	27	26	51	13	33	52	16	42	58	61	23	52
101-250	0	0		0	0	-	1	1	104	9	23	145	11	29	157	21	8	149
251-500	0	0	-	0	0	-	2	2	266	1	3	252	3	8	385	6	2	323
501-1000	0	0	-	0	0	-	0	0	-	0	0	-	1	3	543	1	0	543
1001 and Over	0	0	-	0	0	-	0	0	-	0	0	-	1	3	5102	1	0	5102
Total #	39	100	6	49	100	12	105	100	27	39	100	62	38	100	251	270	100	58

TABLE A-13
TOTAL NUMBER OF PROFESSIONAL PURCHASING PERSONNEL, BY INDUSTRY GROUP

Industry Group	25 or Less			26-100			101-250			251-500			501-1000			1001 Over			Total		
	#	%	Average	#	%	Average	#	%	Average	#	%	Average	#	%	Average	#	%	Average	#	%	Average
Aerospace	7	28	14	9	36	73	12	145	2	8	318	3	12	671	1	4	1054	25	100	196	
Apparel	4	100	14	0	0	-	0	0	-	0	0	-	0	0	-	0	0	-	4	100	14
Chemicals	9	30	8	13	43	52	5	17	127	2	7	331	1	3	530	0	0		30	100	86
Electronic	19	40	12	15	31	53	7	15	196	5	10	348	1	2	800	1	2	1047	48	100	124
Fabricated Metal	1	33	8	0	0	-	2	67	146	0	0	-	0	0	-	0	0	-	3	100	100
Food	16	74	13	5	23	35	1	5	170	0	0	-	0	0	-	0	0	-	22	100	25
Furniture	1	100	11	0	0	-	0	0	-	0	o	-	0	0	-	0	0	-	1	100	11
Industrial Machinery	2	50	9	2	50	48	0	0	-	0	0	-	0	0	-	0	0	-	4	100	28
Instruments	1	50	1	1	50	68	0	0	-	0	0	-	0	0	-	0	0	-	2	100	35
Lumber	1	25	8	3	75	43	0	0	-	0	0	-	0	0	-	0	0	-	4	100	34
Miscellaneous Manufacturing	5	72	5	1	14	29	1	14	227	0	0	-	0	0	-	0	0	-	7	100	40
Paper	12	60	14	6	30	58	1	5	210	0	0	-	1	5	580	0	0	-	20	100	65
Petroleum	5	26	11	9	48	60	4	21	155	0	0	-	1	5	575	0	0	-	19	100	94
Primary Metal	7	54	12	6	46	46	0	0	-	0	0	-	0	0	-	0	0	-	13	100	28
Printing	3	75	12	1	25	41	0	0	-	0	0	-	0	0	-	0	0	-	4	100	20
Rubber	2	100	13	0	0	-	0	0	-	0	0	-	0	0	-	0	0	-	2	100	13
Stone	0	0	-	1	50	55	0	0	-	1	50	380	0	0	-	0	0	-	2	100	218
Textile	3	100	5	0	0	-	0	0	-	0	0	-	0	0	-	0	0	-	3	100	5
Tobacco	2	100	18	0	0	-	0	0	-	0	0	-	0	0	-	0	0	-	2	100	18
Transportation	2	18	20	4	36	43	1	9	127	4	37	401	0	0	-	0	0	-	11	100	177
MANUFACTURING #	102	45	12	76	34	53	25	11	163	14	6	359	7	3	642	2	1	1051	226	100	93
Services	33	49	12	22	34	44	6	9	167	5	7	346	1	1	750	0	0	-	67	100	72
Total #	135	46	12	98	33	51	31	11	164	19	6	355	8	3	656	2	1	1051	293	100	88

TOTAL NUMBER OF SUPPORT PERSONNEL, BY INDUSTRY GROUP

Industry Name	25 or Less			26-100			101-250			251-500			501-1000			1001 Over			Total		
	#	%	Average	#	%	Average	#	%	Average	#	%	Average	#	%	Average	#	%	Average	#	%	Average
Aerospace	14	56	13	8	32	54	1	4	153	1	4	320	0	0	-	1	4	5102	25	100	247
Apparel	4	100	8	0	0	-	0	0	-	0	0	-	0	0	-	0	0	-	4	100	8
Chemicals	14	54	10	6	23	54	5	19	161	1	4	279	0	0	-	0	0	-	26	100	60
Electronics	29	64	7	9	20	58	4	9	177	2	4	418	1	2	543	0	0	-	45	100	63
Fabricated Metal	1	50	7	0	0	-	0	0	-	1	50	253	0	0	-	0	0	-	2	100	130
Food and Beverage	18	86	7	3	14	60	0	0	-	0	0	-	0	0	-	0	0	-	21	100	15
Furniture and Fixtures	1	100	2	0	0	-	0	0	-	0	0	-	0	0	-	0	0	-	1	100	2
Instruments	2	100	4	0	0	-	0	0	-	0	0	-	0	0	-	0	0	-	2	100	4
Lumber and Wood	4	100	15	0	0	-	0	0	-	0	0	-	0	0	-	0	0	-	4	100	15
Machinery, except Electrical	3	75	5	1	25	26	0	0	-	0	0	-	0	0	-	0	0	-	4	100	10
Miscellaneous Manufacturing	6	86	7	0	0	-	1	14	246	0	0	-	0	0	-	0	0	-	7	100	41
Paper	10	53	9	7	37	52	2	11	120	0	0	-	0	0	-	0	0	-	19	100	37
Petroleum and Coal	8	47	7	8	47	40	1	6	125	0	0	-	0	0	-	0	0	-	17	100	30
Primary Metals	9	82	7	1	9	54	1	9	102	0	0	-	0	0	-	0	0	-	11	100	20
Printing and Publishing	3	75	7	1	25	45	0	0	-	0	0	-	0	0	-	0	0	-	4	100	17
Rubber and Plastics	1	100	3	0	0	-	0	0	-	0	0	-	0	0	-	0	0	-	1	100	3
Stone, Clay and Glass	0	0	-	1	50	35	1	50	110	0	0	-	0	0	-	0	0	-	2	100	73
Textile	3	100	10	0	0	-	0	0	-	0	0	-	0	0	-	0	0	-	3	100	10
Tobacco products	2	100	13	0	0	-	0	0	-	0	0	-	0	0	-	0	0	-	2	100	13
Transportation Equipment	4	44	10	3	33	45	1	11	200	1	11	252	0	0	-	0	0	-	9	100	69
MANUFACTURING #	136	65	8	48	23	51	17	9	158	6	3	323	1	0	543	1	0	5102	209	100	66
Services	47	73	10	13	20	58	4	6	113	0	0	-	0	0	-	0	0	-	64	100	26
Total	**183**	**67**	**9**	**61**	**22**	**52**	**21**	**8**	**149**	**6**	**2**	**323**	**1**	**0**	**543**	**1**	**0**	**5102**	**273**	**100**	**57**

TABLE A-15
PURCHASING'S CURRENT ROLE/RESPONSIBILITY/INVOLVEMENT IN MAJOR
CORPORATE ACTIVITIES, AND EXPECTED INVOLVEMENT OVER NEXT 12 MONTHS

	Number of Firms Responding	Percent of Firms in Which Purchasing Has Role/Responsibility/Involvement					Percent of Firms Predicting Change over the next 12 Months		
		% None	% Slight	% Moderate	% Substantial	% Extensive	% Decrease	% Remain Same	% Increase
		%	%	%	%	%	%	%	%
Corporate Strategic Planning	294	10	32	35	18	5	1	60	39
Corporate Mergers/ Acquisitions/Alliances	294	37	33	20	8	2	0	83	16
Technology Planning	293	16	33	40	10	1	2	73	25
Capital Project/ Investment Planning	295	11	28	35	20	6	1	72	27
Marketing Planning	293	33	39	18	10	0	0	77	23
New Product Development	294	16	28	28	21	7	0	65	35
Information Systems Planning	294	8	27	39	21	5	2	58	40
Environmental Planning	294	20	33	33	12	2	0	80	20
Financial/Cash Flow Planning	295	20	33	26	16	5	0	71	28
Risk Management/ Hedging	295	20	32	27	15	6	0	77	22
Government Relations	294	29	40	21	9	1	2	90	8
Outsourcing	292	7	15	27	33	18	0	52	48
International Countertrade/ Offset Planning	291	41	26	19	11	3	1	80	19
Other*	11	18	9	37	18	18	0	62	38

*Other includes: New plant sourcing needs; Services contracting; Reengineering; Consolidation; Shared service centers (Common accts. payables); Manage supplier quality program; Continued development of advanced client/server technology to support contract administration, supplier evaluations, and distributed processing; Quality studies.

CORPORATE HEADQUARTERS' ROLE/RESPONSIBILITY/INVOLVEMENT IN SELECTED ACTIVITIES, AND EXPECTED INVOLVEMENT OVER NEXT 12 MONTHS

	Number of Firms Responding	Percent of Firms in Which Head Office Purchasing Has Role/Responsibility/Involvement					Percent of Firms Predicting Change over the next 12 Months		
		% None	% Slight	% Moderate	% Substantial	% Extensive	% Decrease	% Remain Same	% Increase
		%	%	%	%	%	%	%	%
Contracts for common requirements	283	3	6	16	27	49	4	60	36
Purchases head office requirements	276	9	7	10	23	51	4	80	16
Establishes policies and procedures	280	0	5	11	28	55	3	76	22
Develops supply system, e.g., EDI, credit cards	281	4	12	17	25	41	2	45	55
Participates in system-wide purchasing/supply personnel decisions/actions	283	2	10	16	36	36	1	66	32
Develops and/or provides training	282	5	12	31	28	24	3	65	33
Collects and provides purchasing information	283	2	7	20	36	35	2	63	35
Evaluates/audits unit/divisional performance	278	14	22	27	24	13	3	72	24
Performs special studies and provides reports	281	6	15	32	32	15	2	74	23
Interfaces with government	278	27	39	18	8	8	2	93	5
Interfaces with industry/professional groups/associations	284	1	16	40	31	12	0	84	15
Provides input to and support services for special corporate initiatives in areas such as quality, cost, timeliness, productivity, customer satisfaction	280	3	13	30	34	20	1	67	32
Measures supplier satisfaction	282	10	27	24	20	19	0	66	33
Measures internal customer satisfaction	282	8	17	31	29	15	0	60	39
Participates in interplant purchases and/or goods or services transfers	275	17	24	24	20	15	3	84	13
Others*	25	16	8	8	40	28	7	44	48

*Others include: Supplier/component development; New sources for new plant; Supplier partnership; Renegotiate contracts; Sets continuous process improvement strategy both at supplier and in business office; Systems design and use; Forms management and design; Establish supplier performance standards and participate in perofrmance measurement; Outsourcing; maintains corporate contracts; Manage MRO inventory; Sell idle assets; Manage packaging services; Provides coaching/counseling; Manage outsourced services; Purchase bulk consumables; Develop and implement ISO certified procedures.

TABLE A-17
PURCHASING'S USE OF VARIOUS PURCHASING TECHNIQUES/APPROACHES/ACTIVITIES, AND EXPECTED USE OVER NEXT 12 MONTHS

	Number of Firms Responding	Percent of Firms Using Technique/Approach/Activity					Percent of Firms Predicting Change over the next 12 Months		
		% None	% Slight	% Moderate	% Substantial	% Extensive	% Decrease	% Remain Same	% Increase
		%	%	%	%	%	%	%	%
Purchasing Councils (purchasing managers only)	305	17	22	30	20	11	2	72	26
Supplier Councils (primarily key suppliers)	305	27	30	30	10	3	0	63	38
Commodity Teams (purchasing personnel only)	303	11	23	25	25	16	4	61	35
Cross-functional Teams	307	3	11	30	37	19	0	46	54
Teams involving supplier(s)	306	9	27	39	20	5	0	42	58
Teams involving customer(s)	304	21	30	28	15	6	0	56	43
Teams involving both supplier(s) and customer(s)	304	33	35	20	10	2	0	56	43
Co- location of purchasing personnel with users/specifiers	303	28	23	26	16	7	2	71	27
Consortium buying (pooling with other firms)	306	65	25	7	2	0	0	66	33

TITLE OF CHIEF PURCHASING OFFICER, BY INDUSTRY GROUP

Industry Group	Manager of Purchasing		Director of Purchasing		VP of Purchasing		Materials Manager		Director of Material		VP of Materials Management		Other		Total	
	#	%	#	%	#	%	#	%	#	%	#	%	#	%	#	%
Aerospace	2	7	6	23	2	7	2	7	5	19	3	11	7	26	27	100
Apparel	1	25	1	25	0	0	0	0	0	0	0	0	2	50	4	100
Chemicals	4	13	8	26	3	10	0	0	1	3	4	13	11	35	31	100
Electronics	9	17	10	20	10	20	0	0	7	14	2	4	13	25	51	100
Fabricated Metal	0	0	2	67	0	0	0	0	0	0	1	34	0	0	3	100
Food and Beverage	3	13	2	9	11	48	1	4	0	0	0	0	6	26	23	100
Furniture and Fixtures	0	0	1	100	0	0	0	0	0	0	0	0	0	0	1	100
Instruments	1	50	0	0	0	0	0	0	0	0	0	0	1	50	2	100
Lumber and Wood	0	0	0	0	0	0	0	0	0	0	0	0	4	100	4	100
Machinery except Electrical	1	25	1	25	0	0	1	25	0	0	0	0	1	25	4	100
Miscellaneous Manufacturing	3	44	1	14	1	14	0	0	0	0	1	14	1	14	7	100
Paper	3	15	5	25	5	25	1	5	0	0	2	10	4	20	20	100
Petroleum and Coal	1	5	3	15	0	0	1	5	1	5	0	0	14	70	20	100
Primary Metal	1	7	4	28	2	13	2	13	2	13	2	13	2	13	15	100
Printing and Publishing	0	0	3	75	0	0	0	0	1	25	0	0	0	0	4	100
Rubber and Plastics	1	50	1	50	0	0	0	0	0	0	0	0	0	0	2	100
Stone, Clay and Glass	0	0	0	0	0	0	0	0	0	0	1	50	1	50	2	100
Textile	0	0	1	33	0	0	0	0	1	33	0	0	1	34	3	100
Tobacco Products	0	0	0	0	2	100	0	0	0	0	0	0	0	0	2	100
Transportation Equipment	2	15	5	39	3	23	0	0	0	0	2	15	1	8	13	100
MANUFACTURING #	32	13	54	23	39	16	8	3	18	8	18	8	69	29	238	100
Services	10	14	14	20	14	20	2	3	2	3	2	3	26	37	70	100
Total #	42	14	68	22	53	18	10	3	20	6	20	6	95	31	308	100

TABLE A-19
AGE OF CHIEF PURCHASING OFFICER, BY INDUSTRY GROUP

Industry Group	30-40		41-50		51-60		61 and Over		Total	
	#	%	#	%	#	%	#	%	#	%
Aerospace	3	11	5	19	16	59	3	11	27	100
Apparel	0	0	4	100	0	0	0	0	4	100
Chemicals	2	6	12	39	16	52	1	3	31	100
Electronics	4	8	17	35	26	53	2	4	49	100
Fabricated Metal	0	0	1	33	2	67	0	0	3	100
Food and Beverage	6	26	9	39	8	35	0	0	23	100
Instruments	0	0	0	0	1	50	1	50	2	100
Lumber and Wood	0	0	1	25	2	50	1	25	4	100
Machinery except Electrical	1	25	2	50	1	25	0	0	4	100
Misc. Manufacturing	1	14	1	14	3	43	2	29	7	100
Paper	4	22	7	39	7	39	0	0	18	100
Petroleum and Coal	3	15	5	25	11	55	1	5	20	100
Primary Metal	0	0	8	53	6	40	1	7	15	100
Printing and Publishing	0	0	2	50	2	50	0	0	4	100
Rubber and Plastics	0	0	1	50	1	50	0	0	2	100
Stone, Clay and Glass	0	0	1	50	1	50	0	0	2	100
Textile	1	33	2	67	0	0	0	0	3	100
Tobacco products	0	0	2	100	0	0	0	0	2	100
Transportation Equipment	2	15	4	31	6	46	1	8	13	100
MANUFACTURING #	27	12	84	36	109	46	13	6	233	100
Services	8	12	31	45	28	40	2	3	69	100
Total #	**35**	**12**	**115**	**38**	**137**	**45**	**15**	**5**	**302**	**100**

EDUCATION OF CHIEF PURCHASING OFFICER, BY INDUSTRY GROUP

Industry Group	Highest Education Level							
	High School		Bachelor's Degree		Graduate Degree		Total*	
	#	%	#	%	#	%	#	%
Aerospace	1	4	14	52	12	44	27	100
Apparel	0	0	3	75	1	25	4	100
Chemicals	3	10	14	45	14	45	31	100
Electronics	6	12	28	55	17	33	51	100
Fabricated Metal	0	0	1	33	2	67	3	100
Food and Beverage	0	0	14	61	9	39	23	100
Furniture and Fixtures	0	0	1	100	0	0	1	100
Instruments	0	0	2	100	0	0	2	100
Lumber and Wood	1	25	1	25	2	50	4	100
Machinery except Electrical	0	0	1	25	3	75	4	100
Misc. Manufacturing	1	14	5	71	1	14	7	99
Paper	1	5	8	40	11	55	20	100
Petroleum and Coal	1	5	8	40	11	55	20	100
Primary Metal	1	7	8	53	6	40	15	100
Printing and Publishing	0	0	3	75	1	25	4	100
Rubber and Plastics	0	0	2	100	0	0	2	100
Stone, Clay and Glass	0	0	1	50	1	50	2	100
Textile	0	0	2	67	1	33	3	100
Tobacco products	0	0	2	100	0	0	2	100
Transportation Equipment	0	0	7	54	6	46	13	100
MANUFACTURING #	15	6	125	53	98	41	238	100
Services	2	3	47	67	21	30	70	100
Total #	**17**	**6**	**172**	**56**	**119**	**39**	**308**	**100**

*Totals may not add up to 100 due to rounding.

TABLE A-21
SPECIALIZATION IN BACHELOR'S DEGREE WORK, BY INDUSTRY GROUP

Industry Group	Functional Area								Total	
	Business		Engineering		Liberal Arts		Other			
	#	%	#	%	#	%	#	%	#	%
Aerospace	10	72	3	21	1	7	0	0	14	100
Apparel	2	67	0	0	1	33	0	0	3	100
Chemicals	7	50	4	29	1	7	2	14	14	100
Electronics	14	50	5	18	6	21	3	11	28	100
Fabricated Metal	1	100	0	0	0	0	0	0	1	100
Food and Beverage	9	65	0	0	2	14	3	21	14	100
Furniture and Fixtures	1	100	0	0	0	0	0	0	1	100
Instruments	1	50	1	50	0	0	0	0	2	100
Lumber and Wood	0	0	1	100	0	0	0	0	1	100
Machinery except Electrical	0	0	1	100	0	0	0	0	1	100
Misc. Manufacturing	4	80	0	0	0	0	1	20	5	100
Paper	2	25	3	38	1	12	2	25	8	100
Petroleum and Coal	3	38	4	50	0	0	1	12	8	100
Primary Metal	4	45	0	0	1	11	4	44	9	100
Printing and Publishing	2	100	0	0	0	0	0	0	2	100
Rubber and Plastics	2	100	0	0	0	0	0	0	2	100
Stone, Clay and Glass	1	100	0	0	0	0	0	0	1	100
Textile	0	0	2	100	0	0	0	0	2	100
Tobacco products	1	50	1	50	0	0	0	0	2	100
Transportation Equipment	3	43	2	29	1	14	1	14	7	100
MANUFACTURING #	67	53	27	22	14	11	17	14	125	100
Services	32	70	5	11	7	15	2	4	46	100
Total #	99	58	32	19	21	12	19	11	171	100

THE CHIEF PURCHASING OFFICER: YEARS IN PRESENT POSITION, BY INDUSTRY GROUP

| Industry Group | Years in Present Position | | | | | | | | | | Average Years |
| | 1-5 Years | | 6-10 Years | | 11-15 Years | | Over 15 Years | | Total* | | |
	#	%	#	%	#	%	#	%	#	%	
Aerospace	17	65	8	31	0	0	1	4	26	100	4.58
Apparel	2	50	1	25	0	0	1	25	4	100	7.25
Chemicals	23	74	6	19	0	0	2	6	31	99	4.68
Electronics	31	61	12	24	5	10	3	6	51	101	6.00
Fabricated Metal	1	33	1	33	0	0	1	33	3	99	9.00
Food and Beverage	14	61	6	26	1	4	2	9	23	100	6.43
Furniture and Fixtures	0	0	0	0	1	100	0	0	1	100	12.00
Instruments	0	0	1	100	0	0	0	0	1	100	6.00
Lumber and Wood	1	25	1	25	2	50	0	0	4	100	9.75
Machinery except Electrical	3	75	1	25	0	0	0	0	4	100	3.25
Misc. Manufacturing	2	29	2	29	2	29	1	14	7	101	12.43
Paper	12	60	4	20	1	5	3	15	20	100	6.95
Petroleum and Coal	13	65	4	20	2	10	1	5	20	100	5.10
Primary Metal	11	73	3	20	0	0	1	7	15	100	5.27
Printing and Publishing	2	50	2	50	0	0	0	0	4	100	5.75
Rubber and Plastics	1	50	0	0	0	0	1	50	2	100	16.50
Stone, Clay and Glass	2	100	0	0	0	0	0	0	2	100	3.00
Textile	2	67	0	0	1	33	0	0	3	100	4.67
Tobacco products	1	50	0	0	1	50	0	0	2	100	8.50
Transportation Equipment	7	54	4	31	2	15	0	0	13	100	5.69
MANUFACTURING #	145	61	56	24	18	8	17	7	236	100	6.01
Services	41	60	16	23	12	17	0	0	69	100	5.67
Total #	186	60	72	24	30	10	17	6	305	100	5.93

*Totals may not add up to 100 due to rounding.

TABLE A-23
THE CHIEF PURCHASING OFFICER: YEARS WITH PRESENT EMPLOYER, BY INDUSTRY GROUP

| Industry Group | Years with Present Employer | | | | | | | | | | Average Years |
| | 1-5 Years | | 6-10 Years | | 11-15 Years | | Over 15 Years | | Total* | | |
	#	%	#	%	#	%	#	%	#	%	
Aerospace	2	7	5	19	2	7	18	67	27	100	20.93
Apparel	0	0	1	25	1	25	2	50	4	100	15.50
Chemicals	4	13	6	19	4	13	17	55	31	100	16.32
Electronics	11	22	5	10	8	16	27	53	51	101	17.04
Fabricated Metal	1	33	0	0	0	0	2	67	3	100	16.33
Food and Beverage	0	0	4	18	4	18	14	64	22	100	19.59
Furniture and Fixtures	0	0	0	0	0	0	1	100	1	100	22.00
Instruments	0	0	0	0	0	0	2	100	2	100	31.00
Lumber and Wood	0	0	0	0	1	25	3	75	4	100	22.25
Machinery except Electrical	2	50	0	0	2	50	0	0	4	100	7.0
Misc. Manufacturing	0	0	1	14	1	14	5	71	7	99	25.71
Paper	3	15	4	20	2	10	11	55	20	100	17.35
Petroleum and Coal	0	0	2	10	4	20	14	70	20	100	21.55
Primary Metal	2	13	4	27	0	0	9	60	15	100	16.87
Printing and Publishing	1	25	1	25	0	0	2	50	4	100	16.25
Rubber and Plastics	1	50	0	0	0	0	1	50	2	100	16.50
Stone, Clay and Glass	1	50	0	0	1	50	0	0	2	100	10.00
Textile	0	0	0	0	0	0	3	100	3	100	17.67
Tobacco Products	0	0	0	0	1	50	1	50	2	100	22.00
Transportation Equipment	1	8	2	15	2	15	8	62	13	100	21.46
MANUFACTURING #	29	12	35	15	33	14	140	59	237	100	18.51
Services	13	19	9	13	8	11	40	57	70	100	17.84
Total #	**42**	**14**	**44**	**14**	**41**	**13**	**180**	**59**	**307**	**100**	**18.36**

*Totals may not add up to 100 due to rounding.

THE CHIEF PURCHASING OFFICER : AVERAGE YEARS' EXPERIENCE IN ALL FUNCTIONAL AREAS, BY INDUSTRY GROUP

Functional Area	Aerospace	Apparel	Chemicals	Electronics	Fabricated Metal	Food	Furniture	Machinery except Elec.	Instruments	Lumber	Misc. Manufacturing	Paper	Petroleum	Primary Metal	Printing	Rubber	Services	Stone	Textile	Tobacco	Transportation	Total
Purchasing	18.6	16.5	14.3	17.8	13.0	13.9	23.0	23.0	14.3	8.0	25.7	17.8	11.7	16.7	15.5	24.5	16.3	15.5	5.3	11.5	17.4	16.3
Operations/ Production	5.8	0.8	3.9	4.8	2.3	5.0	0.0	13.5	4.0	3.0	4.1	3.5	5.1	1.7	0.0	5.0	4.7	1.0	12.7	12.5	5.8	4.6
Engineering	1.4	2.5	1.4	1.0	0.0	0.9	4.0	0.0	0.0	0.0	0.0	1.5	1.4	0.4	1.3	0.0	0.6	0.0	0.0	0.0	0.4	0.9
Marketing	0.5	0.0	1.0	1.1	0.3	0.2	0.0	0.0	3.3	0.5	0.4	0.0	2.8	0.5	3.0	0.0	0.6	2.5	0.0	0.0	0.4	0.8
Accounting	0.6	0.0	1.5	0.9	1.0	0.6	0.0	0.0	0.0	0.0	0.0	0.6	0.8	2.7	0.0	0.0	0.8	0.5	0.0	3.0	0.4	0.8
Traffic/Distribu-tion/Logistics	0.3	0.0	0.0	0.4	0.0	0.2	0.0	0.0	0.0	0.0	0.0	0.0	0.5	0.1	0.0	0.0	0.4	0.0	0.0	10.0	0.0	0.3
MIS	0.7	1.3	0.8	0.6	0.0	1.4	9.0	0.0	5.0	0.0	0.0	0.8	1.9	1.2	5.0	0.0	0.8	0.0	6.0	0.0	1.4	1.0
Finance	0.2	0.0	0.0	0.4	11.7	0.2	0.0	0.0	0.0	4.5	0.1	0.7	0.9	1.7	0.0	0.0	0.7	0.0	0.0	0.0	1.0	0.7
Other	2.8	2.5	1.4	0.8	0.0	1.2	0.0	0.0	11.7	3.8	0.0	2.1	2.2	3.1	1.0	0.0	3.2	8.5	1.3	0.0	2.8	2.2
Total Responses	**25**	**4**	**28**	**50**	**3**	**23**	**1**	**2**	**3**	**4**	**7**	**18**	**20**	**15**	**4**	**2**	**69**	**2**	**3**	**2**	**12**	**297**

TABLE A-25
ORGANIZATIONAL RELATIONSHIP DATA BY INDUSTRY

	Aerospace		Apparel		Chemicals		Electronics		Fabricated Metal		Food and Beverage		Furniture and Fixtures		Instruments, Related Products		Lumber and Wood		Machinery except Electrical		Miscellaneous Manufacturing		Paper		Petroleum and Coal		Primary Metal		Printing and Publishing		Rubber and Plastics		Services		Stone, Clay and Glass		Textile		Tobacco Products		Transportation Equipment	
	#	%	#	%	#	%	#	%	#	%	#	%	#	%	#	%	#	%	#	%	#	%	#	%	#	%	#	%	#	%	#	%	#	%	#	%	#	%	#	%	#	%
1. Responding Organizations, 1995 Sales																																										
A. Under $500 Million	7	26	1	25	4	13	10	20	1	34	1	4	1	100	1	50	0	0	2	50	5	72	2	10	0	0	3	20	0	0	0	0	5	7	0	0	0	0	0	0	0	0
B. $0.5 Billion to $1 Billion	5	18	2	50	4	13	7	14	0	0	6	26	0	0	0	0	1	25	1	25	0	0	4	20	6	31	4	27	2	50	2	100	13	19	0	0	2	67	1	50	0	0
C. $1.1 Billion to $5 Billion	7	26	1	25	13	42	18	35	1	33	10	44	0	0	1	50	3	75	1	25	0	0	8	40	0	0	6	40	2	50	0	0	29	43	1	50	1	33	1	50	8	62
D. $5.1 Billion to $10 Billion	4	15	0	0	7	22	7	13	1	33	6	26	0	0	0	0	0	0	0	0	1	14	4	20	3	16	2	13	0	0	0	0	9	13	1	50	0	0	0	0	2	15
E. $10.1 Billion and Over	4	15	0	0	3	10	9	18	0	0	0	0	0	0	0	0	0	0	0	0	1	14	2	10	10	53	0	0	0	0	0	0	12	18	0	0	0	0	0	0	3	23
Total	27	100	4	100	31	100	51	100	3	100	23	100	1	100	2	100	4	100	4	100	7	100	20	100	19	100	15	100	4	100	2	100	68	100	2	100	3	100	2	100	13	100
2. Number of Professional Purchasing Personnel																																										
A. 25 or Less	7	28	4	100	9	30	19	40	1	33	16	73	1	100	1	50	1	25	2	50	5	71	12	60	5	26	7	54	3	75	2	100	33	49	0	0	3	100	2	100	2	18
B. 26-100	9	36	0	0	13	43	15	31	0	0	5	23	0	0	1	50	3	75	2	50	1	14	6	30	9	48	6	46	1	25	0	0	22	33	1	50	0	0	0	0	4	37
C. 101-250	3	12	0	0	5	17	7	15	2	67	1	4	0	0	0	0	0	0	0	0	1	14	1	5	4	21	0	0	0	0	0	0	7	10	1	50	0	0	0	0	1	9
D. 251-500	2	8	0	0	2	7	5	10	0	0	0	0	0	0	0	0	0	0	0	0	0	0	0	0	0	0	0	0	0	0	0	0	4	6	0	0	0	0	0	0	4	36
E. 501-1000	3	12	0	0	1	3	1	2	0	0	0	0	0	0	0	0	0	0	0	0	0	0	1	5	1	5	0	0	0	0	0	0	1	2	0	0	0	0	0	0	0	0
F. 1001 and over	1	4	0	0	0	0	1	2	0	0	0	0	0	0	0	0	0	0	0	0	0	0	0	0	0	0	0	0	0	0	0	0	0	0	0	0	0	0	0	0	0	0
Total	25	100	4	100	30	100	48	100	3	100	22	100	1	100	2	100	4	100	4	100	7	100	20	100	19	100	13	100	4	100	2	100	67	100	2	100	3	100	2	100	11	100
Average Number of Purchasing Professionals:	196		14		86		124		100		25		11		35		34		28		40		65		94		28		20		13		72		218		5		18		177	
3. Number of Support Purchasing Personnel																																										
A. 25 or Less	14	56	4	100	14	54	29	64	1	50	18	86	1	100	2	100	4	100	3	75	6	86	10	53	8	47	9	82	3	75	1	100	47	74	0	0	3	100	2	100	4	45
B. 26-100	8	32	0	0	6	23	9	20	0	0	3	14	0	0	0	0	0	0	1	25	0	0	7	37	8	47	1	9	1	25	0	0	13	20	1	50	0	0	0	0	3	33
C. 101-250	1	4	0	0	5	19	4	9	0	0	0	0	0	0	0	0	0	0	0	0	1	14	2	10	1	6	1	9	0	0	0	0	4	6	1	50	0	0	0	0	1	11
D. 251-500	1	4	0	0	1	4	2	5	1	50	0	0	0	0	0	0	0	0	0	0	0	0	0	0	0	0	0	0	0	0	0	0	0	0	0	0	0	0	0	0	1	11
E. 501-1000	0	0	0	0	0	0	1	2	0	0	0	0	0	0	0	0	0	0	0	0	0	0	0	0	0	0	0	0	0	0	0	0	0	0	0	0	0	0	0	0	0	0
F. 1001 and over	1	4	0	0	0	0	0	0	0	0	0	0	0	0	0	0	0	0	0	0	0	0	0	0	0	0	0	0	0	0	0	0	0	0	0	0	0	0	0	0	0	0
Total	25	100	4	100	26	100	45	100	2	100	21	100	1	100	2	100	4	100	4	100	7	100	19	100	17	100	11	100	4	100	1	100	64	100	2	100	3	100	2	100	9	100
Average Number of Support Personnel:	247		8		60		63		130		15		2		4		15		10		41		37		30		20		17		3		26		73		10		13		69	

	Aerospace #	Aerospace %	Apparel #	Apparel %	Chemicals #	Chemicals %	Electronics #	Electronics %	Fabricated Metal #	Fabricated Metal %	Food and Beverage #	Food and Beverage %	Furniture and Fixtures #	Furniture and Fixtures %	Instruments, Related Products #	Instruments, Related Products %	Lumber and Wood #	Lumber and Wood %	Machinery except Electrical #	Machinery except Electrical %	Miscellaneous Manufacturing #	Miscellaneous Manufacturing %	Paper #	Paper %	Petroleum and Coal #	Petroleum and Coal %	Primary Metal #	Primary Metal %	Printing and Publishing #	Printing and Publishing %	Rubber and Plastics #	Rubber and Plastics %	Services #	Services %	Stone, Clay and Glass #	Stone, Clay and Glass %	Textile #	Textile %	Tobacco Products #	Tobacco Products %	Transportation Equipment #	Transportation Equipment %
4. Organizational Structure																																										
A. Centralized	4	15	0	0	3	10	3	6	1	33	12	52	0	0	1	50	0	0	1	25	5	71	2	10	5	25	4	27	1	25	2	100	22	32	0	0	1	33	1	50	2	16
B. Centralized/Decentralized	15	58	3	75	23	74	42	82	0	0	10	44	1	100	1	50	1	25	2	50	2	29	15	75	14	70	8	53	3	75	0	0	44	65	2	100	2	67	1	50	9	69
C. Decentralized	7	27	1	25	5	16	6	12	2	67	1	4	0	0	0	0	3	75	1	25	0	0	3	15	1	5	3	20	0	0	0	0	2	3	0	0	0	0	0	0	2	15
Total	26	100	4	100	31	100	51	100	3	100	23	100	1	100	2	100	4	100	4	100	7	100	20	100	20	100	15	100	4	100	2	100	68	100	2	100	3	100	2	100	13	100
5. Organization of Firms with Multiple Units																																										
A. Headquarters Purchasing Department Only	0	0	0	0	1	5	6	17	1	34	3	17	0	0	0	0	0	0	0	0	1	33	2	11	0	0	0	0	1	25	0	0	9	19	0	0	1	50			2	25
B. Headquarters Purchasing Department, plus Business Unit Purchasing Department(s)	11	73	1	33	12	54	20	59	1	33	6	33	1	100	1	100	3	75	1	50	2	67	10	56	11	61	6	46	0	0	1	100	21	45	1	50	1	50			3	37
C. Headquarters Purchasing Department, plus Personnel in the Business Unit(s) Who Release Against Contracts	1	7	2	67	6	27	6	18	1	33	9	50	0	0	0	0	0	0	1	50	0	0	2	11	6	33	4	31	3	75	0	0	14	30	1	50	0	0			3	38
D. Headquarters Purchasing Department, but Business Unit Purchasing Department(s)	3	20	0	0	3	14	2	6	0	0	0	0	0	0	0	0	1	25	0	0	0	0	4	22	1	6	3	23	0	0	0	0	3	6	0	0	0	0			0	0
Total	15	100	3	100	22	100	34	100	3	100	18	100	1	100	1	100	4	100	2	100	3	100	18	100	18	100	13	100	4	100	1	100	47	100	2	100	2	100			8	100

TABLE A-25 (Continued)
ORGANIZATIONAL RELATIONSHIP DATA BY INDUSTRY

6. Organization of Firms with Single Units

	Aerospace		Apparel		Chemicals		Electronics		Fabricated Metal		Food and Beverage		Furniture and Fixtures		Instruments, Re-lated Products		Lumber and Wood		Machinery except Electrical		Miscellaneous Manufacturing		Paper		Petroleum and Coal		Primary Metal		Printing and Publishing		Rubber and Plastics		Services		Stone, Clay and Glass		Textile		Tobacco Products		Transportation Equipment	
	#	%	#	%	#	%	#	%	#	%	#	%	#	%	#	%	#	%	#	%	#	%	#	%	#	%	#	%	#	%	#	%	#	%	#	%	#	%	#	%	#	%
A. One Purchasing Department	4	100	1	25	2	40	1	20	2	67	0	0	1	100	1	100			2	100	1	100	2	100	0	0	1	100					8	57			1	100	1	100	3	100
B. Multiple Purchasing Department, But No Headquarters Purchasing Department	0	0			1	20	1	20	1	33	0	0	0	0	0	0			0	0	0	0	0	0	0	0	0	0					1	7			0	0	0	0	0	0
C. Headquarters Purchasing Department, Plus Other Purchasing Department	0	0			2	40	3	60	0	0	2	100			0	0			0	0	0	0	0	0	1	100	0	0					5	36			0	0	0	0	0	0
Total	4	100	4	100	5	100	5	100	3	100	2	100	1	100	1	100			2	100	1	100	2	100	1	100	1	100					14	100			1	100	1	100	3	100

7. Change in Size of Purchasing Organization

	Aerospace		Apparel		Chemicals		Electronics		Fabricated Metal		Food and Beverage		Furniture and Fixtures		Instruments, Re-lated Products		Lumber and Wood		Machinery except Electrical		Miscellaneous Manufacturing		Paper		Petroleum and Coal		Primary Metal		Printing and Publishing		Rubber and Plastics		Services		Stone, Clay and Glass		Textile		Tobacco Products		Transportation Equipment	
	#	%	#	%	#	%	#	%	#	%	#	%	#	%	#	%	#	%	#	%	#	%	#	%	#	%	#	%	#	%	#	%	#	%	#	%	#	%	#	%	#	%
A. Same	5	19	1	25	11	35	23	45			11	50			1	50	2	50	2	50	5	71	11	55	6	30	11	73	1	25	1	50	25	36	1	50	1	33	0	0	6	46
B. Upsized	1	4	1	25	3	10	9	18			1	5			0	0	1	25	0	0	0	0	3	15	3	15	1	7	2	50	0	0	15	22	1	50	0	0	1	50	4	31
C. Downsized	20	77	2	50	17	55	19	37			10	45			1	50	1	25	2	50	2	29	6	30	11	55	3	20	1	25	1	50	29	42	0	0	2	67	1	50	3	23
Total	26	100	4	100	31	100	51	100			22	100			2	100	4	100	4	100	7	100	20	100	20	100	15	100	4	100	2	100	69	100	2	100	3	100	2	100	13	100

TABLE A-25 (Continued)
ORGANIZATIONAL RELATIONSHIP DATA BY INDUSTRY

	Aerospace		Apparel		Chemicals		Electronics		Fabricated Metal		Food and Beverage		Furniture and Fixtures		Instruments, Related Products		Lumber and Wood		Machinery except Electrical		Miscellaneous Manufacturing		Paper		Petroleum and Coal		Primary Metal		Printing and Publishing		Rubber and Plastics		Services		Stone, Clay and Glass		Textile		Tobacco Products		Transportation Equipment	
	#	%	#	%	#	%	#	%	#	%	#	%	#	%	#	%	#	%	#	%	#	%	#	%	#	%	#	%	#	%	#	%	#	%	#	%	#	%	#	%	#	%
8. Change in Organization Size Expected over Next 12 Months																																										
A. Same	10	40	4	100	17	55	24	47	2	67	17	74	0	0	1	50	2	50	2	50	5	72	12	60	11	55	10	66	2	50	2	100	32	47	1	50	3	100	2	100	8	61
B. Upsized	4	16	0	0	6	19	16	31	0	0	4	17	0	0	0	0	2	50	1	25	1	14	5	25	1	5	1	7	2	50	0	0	15	22	1	50	0	0	0	0	1	8
C. Downsized	11	44	0	0	8	26	11	22	1	33	2	9	1	100	1	50	0	0	1	25	1	14	3	15	8	40	4	27	0	0	0	0	21	31	0	0	0	0	0	0	4	31
Total	25	100	4	100	31	100	51	100	3	100	23	100	1	100	2	100	4	100	4	100	7	100	20	100	20	100	15	100	4	100	2	100	68	100	2	100	3	100	2	100	13	100
9. Reporting Relationships of Purchasing																																										
A. President/CEO	5	19	0	0	3	10	9	17	1	34	1	5	0	0	0	0	1	25	1	25	1	15	4	20	2	10	3	20	1	25	0	0	8	12	0	0	1	34	1	50	3	23
B. Executive VP	1	4	0	0	5	17	10	19	1	33	5	23	0	0	1	50	0	0	0	0	0	0	2	10	1	5	2	14	0	0	0	0	14	20	2	100	0	0	1	50	2	16
C. Senior VP/Group VP	3	11	1	25	3	10	5	10	0	0	8	36	1	100	0	0	1	25	1	25	3	43	5	25	0	0	0	0	1	25	1	50	22	32	0	0	0	0	0	0	2	15
D. Administrative VP	3	11	0	0	4	13	1	2	1	33	0	0	0	0	0	0	0	0	0	0	0	0	1	5	6	30	3	20	0	0	0	0	5	7	0	0	0	0	0	0	2	15
E. Financial VP	2	8	0	0	0	0	8	16	0	0	0	0	0	0	0	0	0	0	0	0	0	0	2	10	1	5	2	13	0	0	0	0	8	12	0	0	0	0	0	0	0	0
F. Manufacturing/Production/Operations VP	7	27	2	50	4	13	9	18	0	0	4	18	0	0	1	50	2	50	2	50	1	14	2	10	3	15	0	0	2	50	0	0	3	4	0	0	1	33	0	0	3	23
G. Materials/Logistics VP	1	4	0	0	5	17	5	10	0	0	2	9	0	0	0	0	0	0	0	0	0	0	3	15	0	0	0	0	0	0	1	50	2	3	0	0	1	33	0	0	0	0
H. Engineering VP	1	4	0	0	0	0	0	0	0	0	0	0	0	0	0	0	0	0	0	0	1	14	1	5	1	5	0	0	0	0	0	0	0	0	0	0	0	0	0	0	1	8
I. Other	3	12	1	25	6	20	4	8	0	0	2	9	0	0	0	0	0	0	0	0	1	14	0	0	6	30	5	33	0	0	0	0	7	10	0	0	0	0	0	0	0	0
Total	26	100	4	100	30	100	51	100	3	100	22	100	1	100	2	100	4	100	4	100	7	100	20	100	20	100	15	100	4	100	2	100	69	100	2	100	3	100	2	100	13	100

TABLE A-25 (Continued)
ORGANIZATIONAL RELATIONSHIP DATA BY INDUSTRY

10. Functions Reporting to Purchasing	Aerospace		Apparel		Chemicals		Electronics		Fabricated Metal		Food and Beverage		Furniture and Fixtures		Instruments, Related Products		Lumber and Wood		Machinery except Electrical		Miscellaneous Manufacturing		Paper		Petroleum and Coal		Primary Metal		Printing and Publishing		Rubber and Plastics		Services		Stone, Clay and Glass		Textile		Tobacco Products		Transportation Equipment	
	#	%	#	%	#	%	#	%	#	%	#	%	#	%	#	%	#	%	#	%	#	%	#	%	#	%	#	%	#	%	#	%	#	%	#	%	#	%	#	%	#	%
A. Purchasing	26	100	4	100	31	100	50	100	3	100	23	100	1	100	2	100	4	100	4	100	7	100	20	100	20	100	15	100	4	100	2	100	69	100	2	100	3	100	2	100	13	100
B. Production Scheduling	4	15	1	25	0	0	5	10	0	0	3	13	0	0	0	0	0	0	1	25	1	14	4	20	2	10	0	0	0	0	0	0	4	6	0	0	0	0	1	50	3	23
C. Material Planning	13	50	2	50	7	23	22	44	1	33	9	39	0	0	0	0	2	50	1	25	4	57	9	45	10	50	10	67	2	50	2	100	31	45	0	0	1	33	1	50	5	38
D. Receiving	10	38	1	25	5	16	17	34	1	33	2	9	0	0	0	0	1	25	1	25	4	57	9	45	9	45	9	60	1	25	1	50	32	46	2	100	0	0	2	100	3	23
E. Material & Purchasing Research	13	50	2	50	21	68	26	52	1	33	14	61	1	100	0	0	3	75	1	25	4	57	12	60	15	75	11	73	3	75	1	50	46	67	0	0	2	67	1	50	10	77
F. Stores/Warehousing	9	35	1	25	8	26	19	38	1	33	3	13	1	100	0	0	0	0	0	0	1	14	2	10	13	65	10	67	1	25	1	50	32	46	0	0	1	33	0	0	5	38
G. Inplant Material Movement	5	19	0	0	3	10	13	26	0	0	2	9	0	0	0	0	0	0	0	0	1	14	6	30	4	20	7	47	1	25	0	0	21	30	2	100	0	0	0	0	1	8
H. Inbound Traffic	13	50	2	50	12	39	23	46	3	100	6	26	1	100	0	0	4	100	2	50	1	14	5	25	13	65	13	87	1	25	2	100	41	59	2	100	2	67	0	0	9	69
I. Outbound Traffic	12	46	2	50	9	29	19	38	2	67	1	4	0	0	0	0	0	0	2	50	1	14	16	80	9	45	11	73	1	25	1	50	34	49	0	0	1	33	2	100	7	54
J. Scrap, Surplus Disposal; Inventory Recovery	10	38	2	50	18	58	32	64	1	33	11	48	1	100	0	0	4	100	3	75	6	86	3	15	16	80	14	93	2	50	2	100	38	55	0	0	3	100	0	0	11	85
K. Quality Assurance	6	23	2	50	1	3	14	28	0	0	6	26	0	0	0	0	0	0	1	25	1	14	7	35	9	45	4	27	0	0	0	0	27	39	0	0	1	33	1	50	3	23
L. Inventory Control	10	38	1	25	4	13	21	42	1	33	9	39	0	0	0	0	3	75	1	25	2	29	6	30	12	60	12	80	1	25	1	50	35	51	1	50	1	33	1	50	6	46
M. Other	9	35	1	25	5	16	16	32	0	0	7	30	0	0	0	0	2	50	1	25	0	0	6	30	7	35	0	0	1	25	1	50	22	32	1	50	1	33	1	50	2	15
Total Respondents	26		4		31		50		3		23		1		2		4		4		7		20		20		15		4		2		69		2		3		2		13	

11. Purchasing's Current Role/Responsibility/Involvement in Major Corporate Activities *	Aerospace Index	Apparel Index	Chemicals Index	Electronics Index	Fabricated Metal Index	Food and Beverage Index	Furniture and Fixtures Index	Instruments, Related Products Index	Lumber and Wood Index	Machinery except Electrical Index	Miscellaneous Manufacturing Index	Paper Index	Petroleum and Coal Index	Primary Metal Index	Printing and Publishing Index	Rubber and Plastics Index	Services Index	Stone, Clay and Glass Index	Textile Index	Tobacco Products Index	Transportation Equipment Index
A. Corporate Strategic Planning	2.8	3.3	2.5	2.9	3.0	2.9	4.0	1.0	1.7	2.5	3.0	2.6	2.6	3.1	3.3	4.0	2.6	2.0	3.0	3.0	3.2
B. Corporate Mergers/Acquisitions/Alliances	2.3	2.3	2.3	2.0	3.0	2.3	3.0	1.0	1.7	2.5	1.8	1.6	2.1	2.3	2.0	2.0	1.8	2.5	1.5	2.0	2.3
C. Technology Planning	2.6	3.0	2.3	2.5	2.7	2.7	4.0	1.5	1.3	2.0	3.2	2.1	2.4	2.2	3.0	2.5	2.5	2.0	2.5	2.0	2.4
D. Capital Project/Investment Planning	2.7	3.3	4.3	2.9	3.7	2.7	3.0	1.5	2.3	2.3	3.8	2.7	2.9	3.0	3.5	3.5	2.7	3.5	4.0	2.5	2.8
E. Marketing Planning	2.4	2.5	2.1	2.0	2.3	2.5	3.0	1.5	1.7	2.3	2.0	1.5	1.9	1.9	2.3	2.5	2.1	2.5	1.5	3.5	1.8
F. New Product Development	3.0	3.5	3.0	3.1	3.0	3.7	4.0	2.5	2.0	2.3	3.3	2.0	1.6	1.9	2.8	4.0	2.4	3.0	2.0	3.5	3.6
G. Information Systems Planning	3.3	2.3	3.0	2.9	2.7	3.4	4.0	2.0	2.0	2.5	3.3	2.5	3.1	2.6	3.3	4.0	2.7	3.5	2.0	3.5	3.0
H. Environmental Planning	2.7	1.8	2.6	2.3	2.3	3.0	3.0	2.5	2.0	1.5	3.0	1.8	2.7	2.5	3.0	3.5	2.2	2.5	3.5	2.0	2.0
I. Financial/Cash Flow Planning	3.1	3.0	2.4	2.5	2.5	2.7	5.0	1.0	1.7	2.5	2.3	2.3	2.3	3.1	2.8	3.0	2.3	1.5	3.0	2.5	2.5
J. Risk Management/Hedging	2.8	2.8	2.7	2.1	2.0	3.3	5.0	1.5	1.7	1.8	2.2	2.1	2.3	2.9	2.8	2.5	2.4	2.5	2.0	2.0	2.6
K. Government Relations	3.2	2.3	2.2	3.4	1.7	3.1	3.0	1.0	1.7	1.8	1.5	1.7	2.1	2.2	1.8	2.0	2.1	2.0	1.5	2.5	1.9
L. Outsourcing	4.0	4.0	3.5	3.4	3.0	5.0	5.0	2.5	1.5	3.3	3.3	2.9	3.5	3.1	2.8	4.0	3.4	4.5	2.5	4.0	4.0
M. International Countertrade/Offset Planning	3.3	1.5	2.1	2.3	2.7	2.1	5.0	1.0	1.7	2.5	2.2	1.5	1.8	2.5	1.5	2.5	1.6	2.5	1.0	1.5	2.6
N. Other	—	—	—	3.3	—	5.0	5.0	—	—	—	—	3.0	—	1.0	2.0	2.5	2.5	2.5	—	—	—

* Involvement Index: 1 = None; 2 = Slight; 3 = Moderate; 4 = Substantial; 5 = Extensive

12. Use of Communication Media Between Head Office and Purchasers Elsewhere *	Aerospace Index	Apparel Index	Chemicals Index	Electronics Index	Fabricated Metal Index	Food and Beverage Index	Furniture and Fixtures Index	Instruments, Related Products Index	Lumber and Wood Index	Machinery except Electrical Index	Miscellaneous Manufacturing Index	Paper Index	Petroleum and Coal Index	Primary Metal Index	Printing and Publishing Index	Rubber and Plastics Index	Services Index	Stone, Clay and Glass Index	Textile Index	Tobacco Products Index	Transportation Equipment Index
A. Telephone	4.0	4.3	4.3	4.2	5.0	4.4	4.0	3.0	4.0	3.5	4.8	4.4	4.4	4.3	4.5	4.0	4.3	4.5	4.3	5.0	4.3
B. Letter	2.7	4.0	2.7	2.7	4.0	2.8	3.0	1.0	3.3	2.0	3.3	3.0	2.8	2.7	3.0	2.5	2.7	3.5	3.3	2.0	3.1
C. E-Mail	3.6	2.3	4.1	4.0	3.0	3.4	5.0	3.0	3.0	4.5	2.8	2.7	4.6	2.8	3.3	3.5	3.8	4.5	4.3	5.0	4.0
D. Fax	4.0	3.3	4.1	4.2	4.5	4.1	3.0	3.0	4.3	4.5	4.8	4.1	4.1	4.0	4.0	4.0	3.8	4.5	5.0	5.0	3.8
E. Teleconference	2.9	3.0	3.2	3.4	2.5	3.0	4.0	3.0	2.7	3.5	2.5	2.6	2.8	2.8	3.0	2.0	2.8	3.5	2.5	1.0	3.3
F. Videoconference	2.0	1.0	2.2	2.3	1.0	1.8	1.0	2.0	1.3	1.5	2.0	1.7	2.0	2.1	1.0	2.0	1.9	2.5	2.5	1.0	3.0
G. Personal Meeting	3.1	4.3	2.7	3.2	3.0	2.8	2.0	2.0	3.3	3.0	3.3	2.9	3.3	2.8	2.7	2.5	3.1	3.0	3.5	4.0	3.3

* Involvement Index: 1 = None; 2 = Slight; 3 = Moderate; 4 = Substantial; 5 = Extensive

TABLE A-25 (Continued)
ORGANIZATIONAL RELATIONSHIP DATA BY INDUSTRY

13. Corporate Headquarter's Role/Responsibility/Involvement in Major Corporate Activities *	Aerospace	Apparel	Chemicals	Electronics	Fabricated Metal	Food and Beverage	Furniture and Fixtures	Instruments, Re-lated Products	Lumber and Wood	Machinery except Electrical	Miscellaneous Manufacturing	Paper	Petroleum and Coal	Primary Metal	Printing and Publishing	Rubber and Plastics	Services	Stone, Clay and Glass	Textile	Tobacco Products	Transportation Equipment
	Index	Index	Index	Index	Index	Index	Index	Index	Index	Index	Index	Index	Index	Index	Index	Index	Index	Index	Index	Index	Index
A. Contracts for Common Requirements	3.6	4.3	4.2	4.0	3.3	4.3	5.0	4.0	4.3	3.3	4.2	4.0	4.3	3.8	4.5	5.0	4.3	4.5	4.7	3.5	4.1
B. Purchases Head Office Requirements	3.7	4.0	4.0	3.8	4.0	3.4	5.0	3.0	3.3	4.7	4.2	3.7	6.7	4.5	3.3	5.0	4.3	4.5	4.0	4.5	4.3
C. Establishes Policies and Procedures	4.2	4.5	4.3	4.0	3.3	4.2	5.0	2.0	3.7	3.3	4.5	4.3	4.6	4.6	4.3	4.5	4.6	5.0	4.3	4.0	4.2
D. Develops Supply System, e.g., EDI, Credit Cards	3.8	4.3	4.0	3.7	3.0	3.5	4.0	1.0	3.7	3.7	3.7	3.9	4.4	3.8	4.7	5.0	3.9	5.0	4.3	4.5	3.7
E. Participates in System-Wide Purchasing/Supply Personnel Decisions/Actions	3.8	3.8	3.8	3.7	3.3	4.1	5.0	2.0	2.7	4.0	4.0	3.7	4.2	3.6	3.5	4.5	4.3	4.5	4.3	3.5	3.8
F. Develops and/or Provides Training	3.5	4.0	3.6	3.6	3.0	3.3	4.0	1.0	2.3	3.3	4.3	3.2	3.9	3.5	2.8	4.0	3.6	4.0	2.7	4.5	3.4
F. Develops and/or Provides Training	3.8	3.5	3.7	4.0	4.0	4.1	3.0	2.0	3.7	3.3	4.3	3.8	4.4	4.1	4.0	3.5	4.1	4.0	4.3	3.5	3.8
G. Collects and Provides Purchasing Information	3.5	2.8	3.0	2.7	3.0	3.0	4.0	1.0	2.3	3.0	3.7	2.7	3.1	3.0	3.3	3.0	3.1	4.0	3.0	3.5	2.8
H. Evaluates/Audits Unit/Divisional Performance	3.5	3.0	3.2	3.3	3.7	3.5	5.0	1.0	3.3	3.0	3.3	3.2	3.5	3.4	3.0	3.5	3.4	4.0	4.0	3.5	3.4
I. Performs Special Studies and Provides Reports	3.4	2.5	2.2	2.2	1.3	2.4	4.0	1.0	2.3	2.7	2.5	1.8	2.1	2.4	1.5	1.5	2.3	2.0	2.0	2.0	2.4
J. Interfaces with Government	3.5	3.3	3.2	3.2	2.7	3.5	5.0	1.0	4.0	2.7	3.7	2.9	3.6	3.1	3.5	2.5	3.5	3.5	3.7	3.0	3.5
K. Interfaces with Industry/Professional Groups/Associations	3.6	3.5	3.5	3.5	3.7	3.9	4.0	2.0	3.0	3.3	4.2	3.4	3.1	3.8	3.7	3.5	3.7	3.0	3.7	3.0	3.6
L. Provides Input to and Support Services for Special Corporate Initiatives in Areas Such as Quality, Cost, Timeliness, Productivity, Customer Satisfaction	3.1	3.8	3.2	2.9	1.7	3.6	5.0	1.0	2.7	3.3	3.0	2.8	2.7	3.5	3.5	3.5	3.2	3.5	4.0	4.0	2.8
M. Measures Supplier Satisfaction	3.4	3.3	3.1	3.0	1.7	3.6	3.0	1.0	3.3	2.3	3.8	2.8	3.4	3.4	3.3	4.0	3.5	4.0	4.0	4.0	2.8
N. Measures Internal Customer Satisfaction	2.9	3.0	2.6	3.0	2.3	3.2	5.0	1.0	2.0	2.7	2.7	2.5	3.4	3.3	2.5	3.5	2.8	3.5	4.0	3.0	2.6
O. Participates in Interplant Purchases and/or Goods or Services Transfers	5.0	3.0	3.0	3.0	2.3	3.2	5.0	1.0	2.0	2.7	2.7	2.5	3.4	3.3	2.5	3.5	2.8	3.5	4.0	3.0	2.3
P. Others	5.0		4.0	4.2		4.0	5.0					2.8	3.0	4.0	1.0		4.5				2.3

* Involvement Index: 1 = None; 2 = Slight; 3 = Moderate; 4 = Substantial; 5 = Extensive

TABLE A-25 (Continued)
ORGANIZATIONAL RELATIONSHIP DATA BY INDUSTRY

14. Purchasing's Use of Various Purchasing Techniques/Approaches/Activities *	Aerospace	Apparel	Chemicals	Electronics	Fabricated Metal	Food and Beverage	Furniture and Fixtures	Instruments, Related Products	Lumber and Wood	Machinery except Electrical	Miscellaneous Manufacturing	Paper	Petroleum and Coal	Primary Metal	Printing and Publishing	Rubber and Plastics	Services	Stone, Clay and Glass	Textile	Tobacco Products	Transportation Equipment
	Index	Index	Index	Index	Index	Index	Index	Index	Index	Index	Index	Index	Index	Index	Index	Index	Index	Index	Index	Index	Index
A. Purchasing Councils (Purchasing Managers Only)	3.6	2.8	3.0	3.2	3.0	2.1	3.0	2.0	2.3	2.0	2.8	2.6	2.7	2.9	3.8	2.0	2.6	3.5	2.7	1.5	3.5
B. Supplier Councils (Primarily Key Suppliers)	2.7	3.0	2.1	2.4	2.0	2.4	3.0	2.0	1.5	2.0	2.4	1.8	2.2	2.3	2.5	2.0	2.3	2.5	2.3	1.5	2.9
C. Commodity Teams (Purchasing Personnel Only)	3.5	3.5	2.8	3.5	4.7	3.3	4.0	2.0	3.0	2.8	2.7	2.7	3.0	3.0	3.5	3.0	2.8	3.5	2.3	3.5	2.9
D. Cross-Functional Teams	3.9	3.8	3.8	3.6	2.7	3.8	4.0	2.0	2.5	3.5	2.7	3.4	3.9	3.7	3.3	4.0	3.3	3.5	3.0	3.5	3.6
E. Teams Involving Supplier(s)	2.9	3.3	2.9	2.9	2.7	3.5	3.0	1.0	2.0	2.8	2.1	2.4	2.9	2.9	3.0	2.0	2.8	3.0	3.0	3.5	3.8
F. Teams Involving Customer(s)	2.4	2.0	2.5	2.2	3.0	2.4	2.0	1.0	2.8	1.8	2.5	2.0	3.3	2.5	3.0	3.0	3.0	3.5	2.0	3.5	3.5
G. Teams Involving Both Supplier(s) and Customer(s)	2.1	1.5	2.0	1.8	2.3	2.0	2.0	1.5	1.5	1.5	2.0	1.5	2.6	2.1	3.0	1.5	2.5	2.5	2.0	3.5	1.9
H. Co- Location of Purchasing Personnel with Users/Specifiers	3.0	2.5	2.6	2.4	2.3	2.1	2.0	2.0	3.0	2.5	2.2	1.9	2.8	2.8	3.3	3.0	2.5	4.0	2.0	1.5	2.8
I. Consortium Buying (Pooling with Other Firms)	1.7	1.5	1.4	1.4	2.0	1.7	2.0	1.0	1.5	1.5	1.2	1.3	1.6	1.3	1.8	1.0	1.6	2.5	1.0	1.0	1.3

* Involvement Index: 1 = None; 2 = Slight; 3 = Moderate; 4 = Substantial; 5 = Extensive

	Aerospace		Apparel		Chemicals		Electronics		Fabricated Metal		Food and Beverage		Furniture and Fixtures		Instruments, Related Products		Lumber and Wood		Machinery except Electrical		Miscellaneous Manufacturing		Paper		Petroleum and Coal		Primary Metal		Printing and Publishing		Rubber and Plastics		Services		Stone, Clay and Glass		Textile		Tobacco Products		Transportation Equipment	
	#	%	#	%	#	%	#	%	#	%	#	%	#	%	#	%	#	%	#	%	#	%	#	%	#	%	#	%	#	%	#	%	#	%	#	%	#	%	#	%	#	%
15. The Chief Purchasing Officer																																										
1. Purchasing Agent	2	8	1	25	4	13	9	18	0	0	3	13	0	0	1	50	0	0	1	25	3	43	3	15	1	5	1	7	0	0	1	50	10	14	0	0	0	0	0	0	2	15
2. Manager of Purchasing	6	22	1	25	8	26	10	19	2	67	2	9	1	100	0	0	0	0	1	25	1	15	5	25	3	15	4	27	3	75	1	50	14	20	0	0	1	34	0	0	5	39
3. Director of Purchasing	2	7	0	0	3	10	10	20	0	0	11	48	0	0	0	0	0	0	0	0	1	14	5	25	0	0	2	14	0	0	0	0	14	20	0	0	0	0	2	100	3	23
4. VP of Purchasing	2	7	0	0	0	0	0	0	0	0	1	4	0	0	0	0	0	0	1	25	0	0	1	5	1	5	2	13	0	0	0	0	0	0	0	0	0	0	0	0	0	0
5. Materials Manager	0	0	0	0	0	0	0	0	0	0	0	0	0	0	0	0	0	0	0	0	0	0	0	0	1	5	2	13	1	25	0	0	2	3	0	0	1	33	0	0	0	0
6. Director of Materials	5	19	0	0	1	3	7	14	0	0	0	0	0	0	0	0	0	0	0	0	1	14	0	0	0	0	2	13	0	0	0	0	2	3	1	50	0	0	0	0	0	0
7. VP of Materials Management	3	11	0	0	4	13	2	4	1	33	0	0	0	0	0	0	0	0	0	0	1	14	2	10	0	0	0	0	0	0	0	0	2	3	0	0	0	0	0	0	2	15
8. Other	7	26	2	50	11	35	13	25	0	0	6	26	0	0	1	50	4	100	1	25	1	14	4	20	14	70	2	13	0	0	0	0	26	37	1	50	1	33	0	0	1	8
Total	27	100	4	100	31	100	51	100	3	100	23	100	1	100	2	100	4	100	4	100	7	100	20	100	20	100	15	100	4	100	2	100	70	100	2	100	3	100	2	100	13	100
B. Age																																										
1. 30-40	3	11	0	0	2	6	6	12	0	0	6	26	0	0	0	0	0	0	1	25	1	14	4	22	3	15	0	0	0	0	0	0	8	12	0	0	1	33	0	0	2	15
2. 41-50	5	19	4	100	12	39	17	35	1	33	9	39	0	0	0	0	1	25	2	50	1	14	7	39	5	25	8	53	2	50	1	50	31	45	1	50	2	67	2	100	4	31
3. 51-60	16	59	0	0	16	52	26	53	2	67	8	35	1	100	1	50	2	50	1	25	3	43	7	39	11	55	6	40	2	50	1	50	28	40	1	50	0	0	0	0	6	46
4. Over 60	3	11	0	0	1	3	2	4	0	0	0	0	0	0	1	50	1	25	0	0	2	29	0	0	1	5	1	7	0	0	0	0	2	3	0	0	0	0	0	0	1	8
Total	27	100	4	100	31	100	51	100	3	100	23	100	1	100	2	100	4	100	4	100	7	100	18	100	20	100	15	100	4	100	2	100	69	100	2	100	3	100	2	100	13	100
Average age:	52		45		50		50		52		47		—		60		56		46		53		49		50		51		50		51		50		51		42		46		50	
C. Education																																										
1. High School	1	4	0	0	3	10	6	12	0	0	0	0	0	0	0	0	1	25	0	0	1	14	1	5	1	5	1	7	0	0	0	0	2	3	0	0	0	0	0	0	0	0
2. College Graduate	14	52	3	75	14	45	28	55	1	33	14	61	1	100	2	100	1	25	1	25	5	72	8	40	8	40	8	53	3	75	2	100	47	67	1	50	2	67	2	100	7	54
3. Graduate Degree	12	44	1	25	14	45	17	33	2	67	9	39	0	0	0	0	2	50	3	75	1	14	11	55	11	55	6	40	1	25	0	0	21	30	1	50	1	33	0	0	6	46
Total	27	100	4	100	31	100	51	100	3	100	23	100	1	100	2	100	4	100	4	100	7	100	20	100	20	100	15	100	4	100	2	100	70	100	2	100	3	100	2	100	13	100

TABLE A-25 (Continued)
ORGANIZATIONAL RELATIONSHIP DATA BY INDUSTRY

15. The Chief Purchasing Officer (Continued)

D. Years in Present Position

	Aerospace #	%	Apparel #	%	Chemicals #	%	Electronics #	%	Fabricated Metal #	%	Food and Beverage #	%	Furniture and Fixtures #	%	Instruments, Related Products #	%	Lumber and Wood #	%	Machinery except Electrical #	%	Miscellaneous Manufacturing #	%	Paper #	%	Petroleum and Coal #	%	Primary Metal #	%	Printing and Publishing #	%	Rubber and Plastics #	%	Services #	%	Stone, Clay and Glass #	%	Textile #	%	Tobacco Products #	%	Transportation Equipment #	%
1. 1-5 Years	17	65	2	50	23	74	31	61	1	34	14	61	0	0	0	0	1	25	3	75	2	28	12	60	13	65	11	73	2	50	1	50	41	60	2	100	2	67	1	50	7	54
2. 6-10 Years	8	31	1	25	6	19	12	23	1	33	6	26	0	0	1	100	1	25	1	25	2	29	4	20	4	20	3	20	2	50	0	0	16	23	0	0	0	0	0	0	4	31
3. 11-15 Years	0	0	0	0	0	0	5	10	0	0	1	4	1	100	0	0	2	50	0	0	2	29	1	5	2	10	0	0	0	0	0	0	12	17	0	0	1	33	1	50	2	15
4. Over 15 Years	1	4	1	25	2	7	3	6	1	33	2	9	0	0	0	0	0	0	0	0	1	14	3	15	1	5	1	7	0	0	1	50	0	0	0	0	0	0	0	0	0	0
Total	26	100	4	100	31	100	51	100	3	100	23	100	1	100	1	100	4	100	4	100	7	100	20	100	20	100	15	100	4	100	2	100	69	100	2	100	3	100	2	100	13	100
Average Years in Present Position	4.6		7.3		4.7		6.0		9.0		6.4		12.0		6.0		9.8		3.3		12.4		7.0		5.1		5.3		5.8		16.5		5.7		3.0		4.7		8.5		5.7	

E. Years with Present Employer

	Aerospace #	%	Apparel #	%	Chemicals #	%	Electronics #	%	Fabricated Metal #	%	Food and Beverage #	%	Furniture and Fixtures #	%	Instruments, Related Products #	%	Lumber and Wood #	%	Machinery except Electrical #	%	Miscellaneous Manufacturing #	%	Paper #	%	Petroleum and Coal #	%	Primary Metal #	%	Printing and Publishing #	%	Rubber and Plastics #	%	Services #	%	Stone, Clay and Glass #	%	Textile #	%	Tobacco Products #	%	Transportation Equipment #	%
1. 1-5 Years	2	7	0	0	4	13	11	21	1	33	0	0	0	0	0	0	0	0	2	50	0	0	3	15	0	0	2	13	1	25	1	50	13	19	1	50	0	0	0	0	1	8
2. 6-10 Years	5	19	1	25	6	19	5	10	0	0	4	18	0	0	0	0	0	0	0	0	1	14	4	20	2	10	4	27	1	25	0	0	9	13	0	0	0	0	0	0	2	15
3. 11-15 Years	2	7	1	25	4	13	8	16	0	0	4	18	0	0	0	0	1	25	2	50	1	14	2	10	4	20	0	0	0	0	0	0	8	11	1	50	0	0	0	0	2	15
4. Over 15 Years	18	67	2	50	17	55	27	53	2	67	14	64	1	100	2	100	3	75	0	0	5	72	11	55	14	70	9	60	2	50	1	50	40	57	0	0	3	100	1	50	8	62
Total	27	100	4	100	31	100	51	100	3	100	22	100	1	100	2	100	4	100	4	100	7	100	20	100	20	100	15	100	4	100	2	100	70	100	2	100	3	100	2	100	13	100
Average Years with Present Employer	20.9		15.5		16.3		17.0		16.3		19.6		22.0		31.0		22.3		7.0		25.7		17.4		21.6		16.9		16.3		16.5		17.8		10.0		17.7		22.0		21.5	

F. Average Years Experience in All Functional Areas

	Aerospace Years	Apparel Years	Chemicals Years	Electronics Years	Fabricated Metal Years	Food and Beverage Years	Furniture and Fixtures Years	Instruments, Related Products Years	Lumber and Wood Years	Machinery except Electrical Years	Miscellaneous Manufacturing Years	Paper Years	Petroleum and Coal Years	Primary Metal Years	Printing and Publishing Years	Rubber and Plastics Years	Services Years	Stone, Clay and Glass Years	Textile Years	Tobacco Products Years	Transportation Equipment Years
1. Purchasing	19	17	14	18	13	14	23	23	14	8	26	18	12	17	16	25	16	16	5	12	17
2. Operations/ Production	10	3	12	9	7	10	—	27	6	6	10	9	10	5	—	10	11	2	13	25	14
3. Engineering	7	10	8	7	—	10	4	—	—	—	—	9	7	3	5	—	4	—	—	—	3
4. Marketing	3	—	7	5	1	3	—	—	10	2	3	1	11	2	12	—	4	5	—	—	3
5. Finance	4	—	9	9	3	7	—	—	—	—	—	4	5	21	—	—	6	1	—	6	0
6. MIS	7	—	2	5	—	5	—	—	—	—	—	—	2	2	—	—	6	—	—	20	0
7. Traffic/ Distribution/ Logistics	6	5	6	4	—	11	9	—	15	18	1	5	5	6	20	—	9	—	18	—	4
8. Accounting	5	—	—	6	35	3	—	—	35	15	—	13	4	8	—	—	4	9	—	—	6
9. Other	12	5	5	5	—	5	—	—	—	15	—	4	6	9	4	—	13	—	4	—	17

APPENDIX B •

COVER LETTER AND QUESTIONNAIRE

April 1995

Dear Chief Purchasing Officer:

The first focus study done by CAPS, *Purchasing Organizational Relationships*, 1988, 58 pages, looked at how purchasing is organized, size of staff, to whom it reports, functions it performs, and the background of the CPO. It has been our most-requested study, and we have reprinted it twice. The interest is due, in large part, to the fact that it is the most-current information available on the subject.

We think significant changes have occurred in the past eight years since we collected our original data. Therefore, we are redoing, and broadening, the study, and ask that you complete this questionnaire. It should take less than 15 minutes of your time. We have pretested it personally with the CPOs of eight major firms in Minneapolis and Toronto.

This questionnaire is being sent to three groups of companies:

1. The 297 large firms (less a few who have merged) who provided data for the 1988 study. We will be able to make comparisons between 1988 and 1995.

2. Forty-six large Canadian firms, so we can present a North American picture of how purchasing is organized.

3. An additional 350 large U.S. firms, which have worked with CAPS on past research projects.

While we have identified the questionnaires so that results can be identified by company size and broad industry sectors, CAPS guarantees (and we personally guarantee) that no specific company identifications will be used.

A stamped, return envelope is enclosed. Please return the questionnaire to us by <u>May 12</u>. We thank you in advance for providing the information, which will let us determine how the purchasing function is organized.

Sincerely yours,

Harold Fearon   Mike Leenders
Director of CAPS   Principal Researcher
Principal Researcher

Enclosures: questionnaire and return envelope

CAPS is an affiliation agreement between the College of Business at
Arizona State University and the National Association of Purchasing Management.

CENTER FOR ADVANCED PURCHASING STUDIES
PURCHASING'S ROLES AND RESPONSIBILITIES
April 1995

Please indicate the appropriate responses for you and your firm and return this questionnaire in the attached envelope to:

Center for Advanced Purchasing Studies
PO Box 22160
Tempe, Arizona 85285-2160
(602) 752-2277
FAX (602) 491-7885

NOTE: Your answers to the questions should include people, dollars, and activities that report to the organization headquartered in this country.

1. Size of the firm:
    A. Approximate total annual sales, 1994 (or latest fiscal year) in U.S. dollars.
        _____ under $500 million   _____ $5 billion to $10 billion
        _____ $500 million to $1 billion   _____ $10 billion
        _____ $1 billion to $5 billion

2. What is the title of the chief purchasing officer (CPO) in your firm?
    _____ Purchasing Agent
    _____ Manager of Purchasing
    _____ Director of Purchasing
    _____ Vice President of Purchasing
    _____ Materials Manager (or Materiel Manager)
    _____ Director of Material (or Director of Materiel)
    _____ Vice President of Materials Management (or VP of Materiel Management)
    _____ Other (please give title) _____
    _____

3. Background of the chief purchasing officer (CPO) of the firm:
    A. Age:_____
    B. Education (please check)
        _____ High school graduate
        _____ College graduate (please indicate area of specialization)
            _____ Business
            _____ Engineering
            _____ Liberal Arts
            _____ Other (please indicate)
        _____
        _____ Graduate degree (please indicate degree): _____
        _____
    C. How long has the CPO been in his/her present position?
        _____ years
    D. How long has the CPO been with his/her present employer?
        _____ years
    E. How many total years' experience has the CPO had (total with all present and previous employers), if any, in the following functional areas?
        _____ years in purchasing   _____ years in finance
        _____ years in operations/production   _____ years in management information systems
        _____ years in engineering   _____ years in traffic/distribution/logistics
        _____ years in marketing   _____ years in accounting
                                                      _____ years in other: _____
    F. What was the prior functional area (outside of purchasing) in which the CPO worked and what was the position title?
    Area:_____ Title:_____

    How many years ago was that?_____

4.	To whom does the CPO report?

_____ A.	President/CEO
_____ B.	Executive VP
_____ C.	Senior VP/Group VP
_____ D.	Administrative VP
_____ E.	Financial VP

_____ F.	Manufacturing/production/ operations VP
_____ G.	Materials/Logistics VP
_____ H.	Engineering VP
_____ I.	Other: _____

5.	Which of the following functions/activities are organizationally a part of purchasing (please check all that apply)? If variations within business units occur, please indicate percent in which it is part of purchasing.

_____ A.	Purchasing
_____ B.	Production scheduling
_____ C.	Material planning and control
_____ D.	Receiving
_____ E.	Material and purchasing research
_____ F.	Stores/warehousing
_____ G.	Inplant materials movement
_____ H.	Inbound traffic
_____ I.	Outbound traffic
_____ J.	Scrap, surplus disposal; Investment recovery
_____ K.	Quality assurance
_____ L.	Inventory control
_____ M.	Other (please list) _____

_____

6.	How does your firm organize for purchasing?

_____	Centralized, in which all, or almost all, purchasing is done at one central location for the entire firm.
_____	Centralized/decentralized, in which some purchasing is done at the corporate headquarters and purchasing also is done at major operating divisions/plants.
_____	Decentralized, in which purchasing is done on a division/plant basis.

7.	Indicate the type of purchasing organization:

A.	If your firm is composed of multiple business units, check one below:
_____ 1.	Headquarters purchasing department only.
_____ 2.	Headquarters purchasing department, plus business unit purchasing department(s).
_____ 3.	Headquarters purchasing department, plus personnel in the business unit(s) who release against contracts.
_____ 4.	No headquarters purchasing department, but business unit purchasing department(s).

B.	If your firm is composed of a single business unit, check one below:
_____ 1.	One purchasing department.
_____ 2.	Multiple purchasing departments, but no headquarters purchasing department.
_____ 3.	Headquarters purchasing department, plus other purchasing department(s).

8.	What is the size of the purchasing organization (do not include head count primarily performing related functions such as warehouse, inventory control, production control)?

	Head office	Elsewhere within this country	Elsewhere outside this country
A. Professional purchasing personnel	_____	_____	_____
B. Support staff	_____	_____	_____

9.	In the last 12 months, has your purchasing organization:

_____ A.	Remained the same?
_____ B.	Upsized?	By what percent? _____ %
_____ C.	Downsized?	By what percent? _____ %

Primary reason for change: _____

10.	In the next 12 months, do you expect your purchasing organization to:

_____ A.	Remain the same?
_____ B.	Upsize?	By what percent? _____ %
_____ C.	Downsize?	By what percent? _____ %

Primary reason for change: _____

11. If you have a corporate headquarters (head office) purchasing organization, what term best describes its current role/ responsibility/involvement in:

| | None | Please check one per line | | | | Over the next 12 months, which do you expect to: Please check one per line | | |
		Slight	Moderate	Substantial	Extensive	Decrease	Remain Same	Increase
A. Contracts for common requirements								
B. Purchases head office requirements								
C. Establishes policies and procedures								
D. Develops supply systems, e.g., EDI, credit cards								
E. Participates in system-wide purchasing/supply personnel decisions/actions								
F. Develops and/or provides training								
G. Collects and provides purchasing information								
H. Evaluates/audits unit/ divisional performance								
I. Performs special studies and provides reports								
J. Interfaces with government								
K. Interfaces with industry/ professional groups/ associations								
L. Provides input to and support services for special corporate initiatives in areas such as quality, cost, timeliness, productivity, customer satisfaction								
M. Measures supplier satisfaction								
N. Measures internal customer satisfaction								
O. Participates in interplant purchases and/or goods or services transfers								
P. Other (please indicate):								

12. If your organization has head office purchasing and other purchasers located elsewhere, what use is made of the following communication media between them?

	Please check one per line				
	None	Slight	Moderate	Substantial	Extensive
A. Telephone					
B. Letter					
C. E-mail					
D. Fax					
E. Teleconference					
F. Videoconference					
G. Personal meeting					

13. In performing the purchasing function, what use does your firm make of:

	Please check one per line					Over the next 12 months, which do you expect to: Please check one per line		
	None	Slight	Moderate	Substantial	Extensive	Decrease	Remain Same	Increase
A. Purchasing Councils (purchasing managers only)								
B. Supplier Councils (primarily key suppliers)								
C. Commodity Teams (purchasing personnel only)								
D. Cross-functional teams								
E. Teams involving supplier(s)								
F. Teams involving customer(s)								
G. Teams involving both supplier(s) and customer(s)								
H. Co-location of purchasing personnel with users/specifiers								
I. Consortium buying (pooling with other firms)								

14. In your firm which term would best describe purchasing's current role/responsibility/involvement in major corporate activities:

	None	Slight	Moderate	Substantial	Extensive	Decrease	Remain Same	Increase
		Please check one per line				Over the next 12 months, which do you expect to: Please check one per line		
A. Corporate Strategic Planning								
B. Corporate Mergers/ Acquisitions/Alliances								
C. Technology Planning								
D. Capital Project/ Investment Planning								
E. Marketing Planning								
F. New Product Development								
G. Information Systems Planning								
H. Environmental Planning								
I. Financial/Cash Flow Planning								
J. Risk Management/ Hedging								
K. Government Relations								
L. Outsourcing								
M. International Countertrade/ Offset Planning								
N. Other (please indicate):								

15. By the year 2001, in your firm what major innovation/change in purchasing organization would contribute significantly to organizational effectiveness?

_____

_____

_____

_____

Thank you for completing the questionnaire. We will send you a copy of the completed study (estimated completion August 1995). Should you wish to talk with either researcher in advance of completion of the study, please call: Mike Leenders (519) 661-3284, or Hal Fearon (602) 752-2277.

CENTER FOR ADVANCED PURCHASING STUDIES •

THE CENTER FOR ADVANCED PURCHASING STUDIES (CAPS) was established in November 1986 as the result of an affiliation agreement between the College of Business at Arizona State University and the National Association of Purchasing Management. It is located at The Arizona State University Research Park, 2055 East Centennial Circle, P.O. Box 22160, Tempe, Arizona 85285-2160 (Telephone [602] 752-2277).

The Center has three major goals to be accomplished through its research program:

to improve purchasing effectiveness and efficiency;
to improve overall purchasing capability;
to increase the competitiveness of U.S. companies in a global economy.

Research published includes 24 focus studies on purchasing/materials management topics ranging from purchasing organizational relationships to CEOs' expectations of the purchasing function, as well as benchmarking reports on purchasing performance in 26 industries.

Research under way includes: *Measuring Purchasing Effectiveness; Purchasing Futures Study; Purchasing Consortiums*; and the benchmarking reports of purchasing performance by industry.

CAPS, affiliated with two 501 (c) (3) educational organizations, is funded solely by tax-deductible contributions from organizations and individuals who want to make a difference in the state of purchasing and materials management knowledge. Policy guidance is provided by the Board of Trustees consisting of: